LEMURIAN CONNECTIONS:

Using Ancient Wisdom
to
Solve Today's Problems

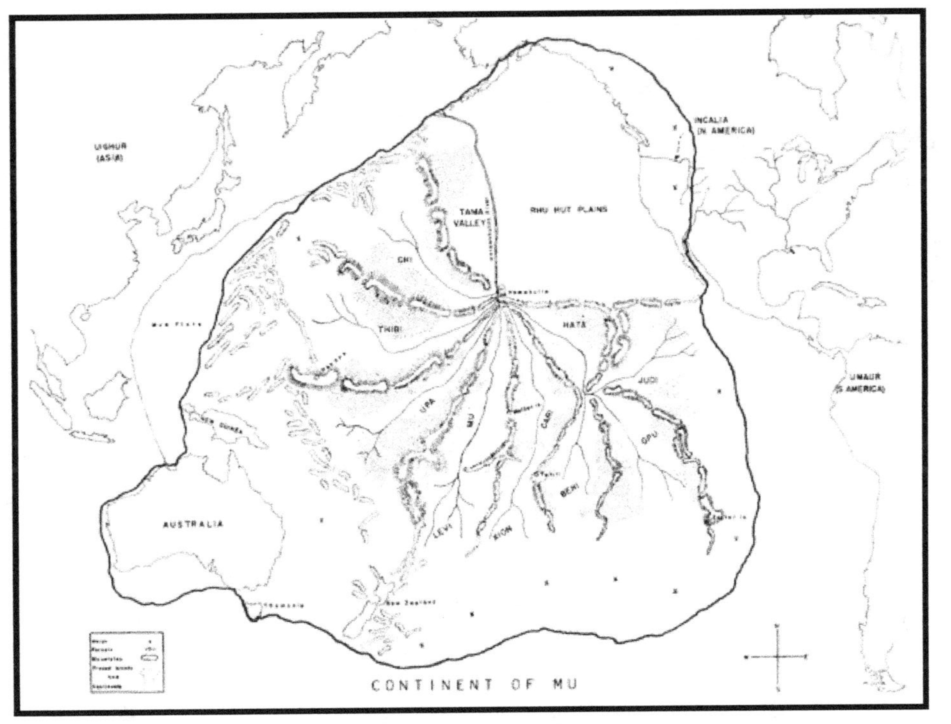

UIGHUR (ASIA)
INCALIA (N AMERICA)
UMAUR (S AMERICA)
TAMA VALLEY
RHU HUT PLAINS
CHI
HATA
THIBI
JUDI
OPU
UPA
CAR
BEKI
LEVI
KION
AUSTRALIA
NEW GUINEA
New Zealand
CONTINENT OF MU

Lemurian Connections: *Using Ancient Wisdom to Solve Today's Problems*

To learn more about the Lemurian Fellowship's work, please contact them through their website:

https://www.lemurianfellowship.org/

Library of Congress Cataloging-in-Publication Data
Lemurian Fellowship

Lemurian Connections: *Using Ancient Wisdom to Solve Today's Problems*

ISBN: # 9781513653273 (paperback)
ISBN: # 9781513653280 (eBook)

1. OCC031000 **BODY, MIND & SPIRIT**/Ancient Mysteries & Controversial Knowledge **2.** (OCC019000 **BODY, MIND & SPIRIT** / Inspiration & Personal Growth **3.** SEL016000 **SELF-HELP**/Personal Growth/ Happiness

Empowered Whole Being Press
www.EmpoweredWholeBeingPress.com

Table of Contents

Introduction

Are *you* a Lemurian? Or do you have an inner feeling that you *were* a Lemurian in the long-forgotten days when Lemuria or Mukulia was not only a great civilization, but an Empire?

Fifty years ago, many of those who found their way to the Lemurian Fellowship came to ask, "What *is* Lemuria?" Now it's a rare person who hasn't heard something about this mythical land that has inspired books, movies, and even a comic strip that debuted in the 1930s.

An idea with such a hold on the human imagination must have some basis. Is it possible that the suggestion of a prehistoric civilization that flourished for thousands of years could stir long-forgotten *memories* of our own lives there?

Robert D. Stelle, the founder of the Lemurian Fellowship, was an unusual man who became interested in this question long before the idea of Lemuria captured the popular imagination. He was contacted by more highly advanced men and women known as Masters, who helped and encouraged him in his efforts to learn more that could help people everywhere. When he learned that the Lemurians developed the most nearly perfect civilization Earth has known, he realized how vital it was to help others understand how this was possible so we, too, could create a society where everyone could benefit, not just the few.

This book, comprised of personal experiences written by Lemurian Fellowship teachers and students, talks about Lemurian life today as well as glimpses into Lemurian history taken from Dr. Stelle's book, *The Sun Rises*. It reveals information about the Masters who guide and direct the Fellowship, and experiences from Lemurian students' lives, showing how the Philosophy can help any of us make positive changes and create a sphere of positive protection around ourselves in this rapidly changing, uncertain world.

To learn more about the Lemurian Fellowship please visit our website, lemurianfellowship.org, email us at office@lemurianfellowship.org or call the Fellowship at 760-789-1420.

ANCIENT WISDOM

We're All One in God's World

With the extreme conditions we are seeing more and more often, people everywhere long for reassurance and peace, and "We're all one" may seem like a distant dream. So may it bring hope to consider that, with the core of goodness inside so much of humankind, a more inclusive and positive future is not only urgently needed, but entirely achievable. No matter where we live or what our beliefs, all of us have a common basis in the desire for freedom, security, and peace of mind. We're all one, as reflected so well in the expression of the Golden Rule in seven world religions:

Christianity – "All things whatsoever ye would that men should do to you, do ye even so to them."

Confucianism – "Do not unto others what you would not they should do to you."

Buddhism – "In five ways should a clansman minister to his friends and familiars – by generosity, courtesy and benevolence, by treating them as he treats himself, and by being as good as his word."

Hinduism – "Do not to others, which if done to thee would cause thee pain."

Islam – "No one of you is a believer until he loves for his brother what he loves for himself."

Judaism – "What is hurtful to yourself, do not to your fellow man."

Taoism – "Regard your neighbor's gain as your own gain and regard your neighbor's loss as your own loss."

With this universal principle as a basis, and to help bring us together in friendship and harmony, wise and understanding Masters have supplied the essential information we need in the Lemurian Philosophy. It is based on principles that apply to all people, no matter what race, color, or belief. Within it are plans for a magnificent program that will culminate in *the Kingdom of God* – a civilization that must first be built within each of us with every kind and positive thought and action. Within it, all will live and work together in harmony and for the greatest good of all, knowing that only in this way may they earn these spiritual treasures for themselves.

If this sounds like a Utopian scheme to you, you may be encouraged to know that Lemurian principles have been used before to build a harmonious civilization that endured for thousands of years. And as we begin to transmute our present civilization into a more ideal one, Lemurian students have been living and working together using these principles in Southern California for over sixty years. They are proving the validity and efficacy of this way of life and are actively earning a place in the coming civilization. You can too!

May you be reassured by the thought that we're all one and affected by each other whether near or far. As we take hold of the guidance of those greater than ourselves, together we can build a more peaceful today and work together for a better tomorrow.

Confucius: One of the Great Ones We Honor

About 500 years before the Advent of Christ, a great wave of spiritual illumination swept the world. Some of the greatest religious and moral teachers – Confucius and Lao-Tse in China, Buddha in India, Zoroaster in Persia, Socrates and Plato in Greece – incarnated nearly simultaneously and their accomplishments were phenomenal. Doesn't this seem like the outworking of a farseeing plan to prepare the way for Christ?

Confucius (Kung-fu-tze) may have had more influence over more people for a longer time than anyone other than Christ. His philosophy, laws, and literature became Chinese national classics. Every city and town had shrines for this revered teacher and inspired sage. His precepts influenced the social customs and religious thinking of millions of Chinese for 2,400 years.

A shrewd teacher, facile in his opinions and questions, he was never known to argue. By 30, his fame attracted students from all over the country and brought him three thousand disciples. Feeling ordained to teach government and morals to humanity, he looked for employment at the courts, but most princes would not accept him. Though this seemed a failure, he had great confidence in himself and his mission. He wouldn't change his rules and principles yet admitted that "I am a transmitter and not a maker, believing in and loving the ancients. I am not virtuous enough to be free from anxiety, not wise enough to be free from perplexities, and not bold enough to be free from fears."

Confucius taught that human nature is good and can be developed to perfection. He said the superior person conquers and cultivates life to rise above all its littleness and master himself, yet never claimed he had reached that point. He emphasized our tendency to kindliness, happiness in doing good, desire for justice, hope, and the attraction of higher ideals, saying these are the normal, true ideals of life. Confucius was said to be a lot like Benjamin Franklin in spirit, manners, wisdom and even appearance.

Historian Will Durant, who spent forty years writing the eleven volumes of *The Story of Civilization*, considered the following passage by Confucius the wisest in all literature, as complete a guide to life today as it was to life in China in 500 B.C.:

The ancients who wished to exemplify the highest virtue throughout the empire first ordered well their own states. Wishing to order their states, they first regulated their families. Wishing to regulate their families, they first cultivated their own selves. Wishing to cultivate their own selves, they first rectified their hearts. Wishing to rectify their hearts, they first sought to be sincere in their thoughts. Wishing to be sincere in their thoughts, they first extended to the utmost their knowledge. Such extension of knowledge lay in the solving of problems.

This conforms perfectly to the Lemurian approach to life, where students and Order members work to improve their most pressing problems using the knowledge they have gained by applying Lemurian principles in their lives and affairs. Then each student becomes a building block for the better civilization to come, as Confucius explains:

Problems being solved, knowledge became complete. Knowledge being complete, their thoughts were sincere. Their thoughts being sincere, their hearts were rectified. With hearts rectified, their own selves were cultivated. Their own selves cultivated; their families were regulated. Their families regulated; their states were rightly governed. Their states rightly governed, the whole empire was made tranquil and happy.

It is always tempting to speculate on what other incarnations a great Ego may have had. Is it possible Confucius was a later incarnation of another Chi Yan well known to Lemurians? We don't know, but it's interesting to ponder!

Maya Discovery

*Maya civilization was much vaster than known,
thousands of newly discovered structures reveal*

– The Washington Post, February 3rd, 2018

"What does this Maya discovery have to do with the lost continent of Lemuria?" you may ask, and the connection seems quite obscure without the advantage of a little ancient history.

A hundred and twenty years ago the Lemurian Fellowship's founder, Robert Stelle, then just a teenager, was prospecting with two other Americans when they encountered Mayas in southern Mexico. These people were suspicious of strangers and anyone who spoke Spanish, although they understood the language. This put the trio in a difficult spot because English was almost unknown to the Maya, but they managed to make friends by treating them honestly and respecting their customs.

When they were sure these white men wouldn't take advantage of them, the Maya showed them carefully hidden ancient temples, some buried under earth and rubble that had been laboriously carried and poured over them by their ancestors to hide them from the Spanish. Robert and his two companions entered one of these buried buildings, encountering two deadly traps they managed to survive, eventually reaching a room they estimated to be 100 feet long and 60 feet wide, its roof supported by beautifully carved stone pillars. The walls were covered with beautifully painted scenes.

The stone floor, Dr. Stelle recalled years later, showed the wear of long usage, having been worn to a depth of a foot or so where people entered and left the room. Considering the hardness of the stone, that it was protected from the elements, and that the feet passing over it were bare or clad only in soft leather moccasins, we can only guess at the age of this building. How great must have been the population of this area?

When Robert and his friends left this hidden building, they carefully closed the entrance with fresh logs covered with dirt to honor their promise to the Maya not to reveal anything they discovered. From that time until they left the country, the Maya were always friendly and helped them carry their equipment until they could find horses.

Eventually, they came across one old Maya priest who took an interest in the young American. Since Robert had picked up only a few Mayan words, and neither he nor the old man was fluent in Spanish, they used an intelligent young Maya who had lived in Texas as an interpreter. Asking that Robert not discuss what he learned with any local Mexicans, the old man told Robert there had once been a great civilization in the now jungle-covered land. He said the time would come when Robert would be able to reconcile these facts with others he would learn, and then he would reveal them to others, adding, "I shall long since have left the flesh by then, my son, and it is well that this history should be revealed as only you may do it."

Both the old priest and the interpreter had trouble expressing numbers higher than 100, but by using stones to represent ten hundreds, or 1,000, they finally conveyed the time as 46,000 years since the first Mayas, then called Mu Yans, had come to their country as a great army from the "Motherland."

At the time he heard this, Robert knew nothing of the Continent of Mu or Lemuria. But what he heard stayed with him until much later when he was able to weave together all he had gathered through the years into one coherent history, to which the Elder Brothers added much confirming data. Much of this became part of the Lemurian Philosophy, which is available to every sincere Lemurian student, although much also remains in the Fellowship archives for release at a later time, when humankind is readier for it.

WHAT LEMURIA KNEW

So many of our worries, problems, and troubles were unknown to Lemurians during their golden age.

With the help of Great Ones guiding them, ancient Lemurian Elders progressed from making crude pictures to alphabetical characters and soon learned to write. With the civilization's rapid growth, they decided a record should be kept of every discovery and advancement. Under the Great Ones' direction, the Thirteenth School was organized to preserve what Lemuria knew.

Here, every piece of literature, every perfected plan, superior examples of artists' and craftsmen's skill and working models of every invention throughout the fifty thousand years of Lemurian history were carefully preserved. The Thirteenth School kept every detail of the Empire's progress in art, music, invention, scientific discovery and general knowledge. Every step in the operation of cosmic law as it affects human living, including the priceless teachings, opinions and directions given them by Greater Ones, was treasured and maintained here. All these records were studied, analyzed, and cross-indexed, further enhancing the knowledge of those selected to fulfill this responsibility.

With this amazing resource it isn't surprising that the Empire grew so great and its inhabitants lived so well. We are justly proud of our own way of life today with all that science and technology makes possible for us. But imagine every home built with spacious bathing pools featuring varied-colored quartzes, filled with filtered, scented water.

Or kitchens fitted with gem-studded, pure silver and gold fixtures. These noble metals were used because of their long-lasting qualities and resistance to corrosion, since everything in Mukulian times was built for permanence.

Today's most advanced entertainment rooms are only now approaching those of Mukulian families who enjoyed music systems and a form of television as well as being able to see, hear, and talk naturally with their distant friends while seeing them in three-dimensional perspective as naturally as if in the same room. And this was more than thirty thousand years ago!

Surprising as its material progress was, what Lemuria knew about *quality of life* was light years ahead of us. They enjoyed a sense of purpose, happiness, and peace seldom experienced today; a form of universal security hard to describe because we have nothing generally known today that comes close.

Such everyday intrusions and atrocities as bullying, identity theft, muggings, robbery, car-jackings, murder, rape, terrorism or road rage were unknown. For instance, from 40,000 BC to 28,000 BC, a period of 12,000 years, there was no record of theft in the Mukulian Empire. Compare that with the criminal records of any modern city for a single day!

Before the destruction of Mu, the priceless records concerning every discovery, invention, and improvement in living were taken to Asia where they have been guarded by what is now known as the Lemurian Mystery School. What Lemuria knew isn't lost. And in the ages since, these Masters have continued to analyze the successes and failures of every civilization since Mu, from Atlantis, Egypt, and India to the present, to understand how and why cultures succeed or fail.

This wisdom will be released as soon as humanity has brought greed and intolerance under consistent control and people have proven they are ready to use it only for good. Its basics are available today through the Lemurian Philosophy which is once again being taught to those who are sincerely proving the validity of universal principles by *using* them to enhance their own lives and improve our world.

Lemuria's Blue Messengers

Early in the history of Mu, citizenship schools were set up in the tribal valleys. Some way of communicating between them and the Rhu Hut Plains was needed so they could keep up with fast-changing developments in the growing civilization. Since writing was unknown, messages had to be memorized, then spoken to the receiver. These messages were often long and complex, so the carrier had to be more intelligent than average to understand, remember, and repeat what he had been given.

The trip from the capital city of Hamukulia to any of the valley schools was dangerous and as far as thousands of miles. Most of the country was wild, rugged, unmapped and trailless, and all travel was by foot. It would have been easier to walk from what is now Plymouth Rock, Massachusetts to San Diego, California when America was first discovered than to go from Hamukulia to the school in the Levi Valley.

Even though there was more danger from animals at night, messengers usually traveled then because many people in the valleys were savage and there was less danger of being seen. The human sense of smell then was as sharp as that of animals. It had to be, because a man's life depended on being able to smell an enemy, animal or human, when he couldn't see or hear it.

Since night travel was dangerous for the messengers, they began to dye their bodies blue with certain berries and herbs. These took away all traces of the human scent, and the blue stain made the messengers almost invisible in the dark starlit nights. Even when the moon was out they could melt into the shadows.

Because those chosen as messengers were highly intelligent with unusual powers of memory, concentration, physical stamina and endurance, this work was prized. To be a messenger was a great distinction, and each one wanted to raise sons to take over this honored and difficult task. After several generations, there was a peculiar change in these children. The skins of both boys and girls developed a bluish tinge and eventually they were born blue and kept this coloring all their lives.

Training for the honor of becoming a Blue Messenger began in infancy. This training, plus all that was learned from the messages they carried, enabled the Blue Messengers to make rapid mental and spiritual progress.

When Lemuria was at the peak of its glory, ambassadors to other countries were always selected from among Blue Messenger families. Almost every director or even assistant director of the Department of Communication was distinguished by his blue skin. Every Emperor depended on Lemuria's Blue Messengers as ambassadors with the qualities of character and temperament needed to fill these positions. Thousands of years of training qualified them for these positions of great trust where sound judgment and unshakeable integrity were so essential. Distant people came to regard these respected dignitaries from the Motherland as representing what they believed was a blue race.

In time, written communication became common, and later inventions like our radio, television, and more advanced means of communication gradually took the place of physical messengers. But until the collapse of the Mukulian Empire, descendants of Lemuria's Blue People seldom married any but blue partners from other messenger families, protecting their hard-won distinction for thousands of years.

Lemuria and Robert Stelle's Revelations

How did Lemuria and Robert Stelle become so closely associated? What led him to discover artifacts of this long-lost continent, and how did he earn help from the Masters to understand its profound meaning for us today?

Lemuria and Robert Stelle's Discoveries

Robert Stelle was a most unusual boy, with psychic abilities and contacts beginning very early. At 15, Bob joined two explorers in South America. In Chichen Itza, Yucatan, he saw distinctive pyramids that later he found duplicated in other parts of the world. At Cuzco, Peru, he marveled at walls so skillfully built that a knife blade couldn't fit between the stones.

Recent earthquakes had no effect on the old walls, but modern stone additions were destroyed. An old tribal chief in Mexico told him many half-understood things about "the Old Ones from the Motherland." And at Lake Titicaca, 13,500 feet above sea level, he saw stone-lined canals that seemed to serve no purpose. What did it all mean?

Knowing the earth has changed, with ocean fossils found in mountains and sunken cities still visible, Bob reasoned Lake Titicaca was once at sea level when its canals connected the Pacific and Atlantic, before upheavals lifted the Andes Mountains. But why?

His adventures took him to Pohnpei with its ancient ruins of Metalanim. Its walls, temples, and artificial canals cover 11 square miles. It is built of surfaced basalt blocks collectively weighing 750,000 tons. Who built it? Who was it built for?

Scientists claim its people built Metalanim over open water on a coral reef and constructed 92 artificial islands. They admit not understanding how basalt columns were brought there or raised for the walls. They say building Metalanim would have been a greater effort than the Egyptian Pyramids. But Pohnpei is only one-fifth the size of Oahu, Hawaii, and supposedly had fewer than 30,000 people. Does this theory make sense?

Three thousand miles from Pohnpei, Malden Island is barren and uninhabitable, but with forty stone temples like those on Pohnpei, and highways of surfaced basalt blocks disappearing into the ocean. Where did they lead?

Lemuria and Robert Stelle's Revelations

To Robert Stelle, these pieces fit into the puzzle of Lemuria. He kept probing for greater understanding. In China he met a Master who was to work with him for the rest of his life. This wise and learned man helped him become more receptive to clues from the Masters so he could fit the puzzle pieces together, and soon Dr. Stelle contacted others who also helped him.

In 1936, he and an associate established the Lemurian Fellowship and released the Lemurian Philosophy. Masters helped and guided them through years of hard work, sacrifice, and constant refinement of information released clairvoyantly to Dr. Stelle. In 1941 he began writing **The Sun Rises**, about his own experiences in an earlier lifetime. This true history of how the world's first and greatest civilization began took eleven years to complete. Lemuria and Robert Stelle are closely linked for all who seek the truth about this almost forgotten civilization.

Dr. Stelle's experience helps us know that what we accomplish is mostly up to us, but we aren't completely on our own. Help is always close by when we need and ask for it. If we are working on something beneficial for humanity, we attract and earn help from Higher Beings who allow us full use of our minds and initiative so we gain the fullest experience and advancement. This was true at civilization's beginning and is just as true today.

Folk Sayings Echo Ancient Wisdom

*What is wisdom save a collection of platitudes?
Nonetheless, they embody the concentrated experience
of the race, and the man who orders his life according
to their teaching cannot go far wrong.*

– Norman Douglas

Doesn't the wisdom in folk sayings make you feel better? They reaffirm truths we believe in. We like how they capture so much in a few words, laugh at their humor, respond to their poetry. A few minutes with the world's best maxims is like a refreshing dip in a quiet pool after a hectic day.

And what could fit more naturally into the Twitter generation's lifestyle than these short, punchy one-liners? Our craving for catchy sound bites and concise bumper stickers can be soothingly satisfied with a collection of the world's timeless adages.

Even better is the luxury of time to focus on them, digging beneath their obvious observation to the deeper truths they hint at. Truth has many layers, and proverbs that withstand the test of time hold an element of it. There's more to them than meets the eye.

The same truth echoes through different times and places. Christ said, "If any man desire to be first, the same shall be last of all, and servant of all." The Bulgarians: "If you can't serve, you can't rule." And in Yemen, "The master of the people is their servant."

As you sift through these wise words, you realize the most perceptive can be traced to the unusual human beings who uttered them. Some originators are lost in antiquity, so many proverbs are anonymous, or identified only as Chinese, Latin, biblical. But names like Aesop, Socrates, Confucius, Christ, Shakespeare, Lincoln, Franklin, Gandhi, Twain, the Dalai Lama or Mother Teresa crop up enough to make you suspect some wise and learned individuals originated most of these treasures.

Whatever their origin, we are grateful for these pithy reminders of what's good, beautiful, and lasting in our collective experience of the last several millennia. Lemurian students find the wisdom in folk sayings echoes some of the ancient wisdom we study in the Lemurian Philosophy and help us affirm connections we know exist among people everywhere, even when you discover these apparently clear and concise statements of universal truth can be interpreted very differently.

During high school study hall, I dug into a dictionary looking for more obscure sayings. A French one, "a bon chat, bon rat," translated as, "To the good cat, the good rat." I thought this meant something like "The early bird gets the worm." But later, I had a chance to try "a bon chat, bon rat`" on a French speaker. He responded immediately, "Oh yes: 'The cart before the horse'!" (Maybe it was my accent.)

It's true that any two of us may find a different meaning or a new moral, because we each have a unique experience background. And that's where we really start to learn from others.

It's interesting and just plain fun to talk over these sayings together, compare our own experiences with the truths they convey, drawing closer in our understanding of each other. You will find them scattered through these blog articles and related to the universal principles they encode. We hope you enjoy this mental and spiritual recreation as much as we do. Send us one of your favorite quotes!

What Is God and Where Do I Find God?

A young man wrote the Fellowship asking, "What is God and where do I find God?" A vital question to ask as we continue our spiritual journey this lifetime!

Christ said two laws are more important than all others: to love God with all our heart and with all our being, and to love our fellow human beings as we love ourselves. These are the twin paths to knowing God. Believing in and loving God is one path that leads naturally to loving others. Or we may begin with our love of others and through this, find God.

Many of us have an innate sense of a higher power, a greater Intelligence behind the orderly operation of the universe and the events of our lives. But those who question or doubt need some help to reason toward this understanding, and as they make this effort, their faith grows stronger.

The truth that God is good is a starting point. Those who recognize God's presence in themselves, whether Christian, Muslim, Jewish, Buddhist, or any God-centered faith, have one universal quality in common. They've learned to recognize that all we do either reflects God or it doesn't. They've learned things they can do that reflect God more strongly in themselves.

In a family, marriage, or with friends, we often do unselfish things for each other. Have you noticed how your love for someone deepens when they perform some kindness for you? And haven't you done things for them just to see the joy on their faces and experience the happiness this brings?

Sometimes, the depth of this love becomes most evident when someone you love dies. You know the ache of losing them, the feelings of loss. Having someone you can freely give your kindness and love to is priceless. You love being able to share yourself, your deepest thoughts, your dreams with someone close. You could do this with anyone, but there are some with whom these feelings have grown over time, so instead of spreading these acts of love to all we meet, we reserve them for those we trust to respect them. By doing this, do we limit our expression of God, and thereby, our recognition of God?

When children leave home for the first time, unless they have learned to reach out easily to others, there will be a noticeable hole in their lives. It will be a lonely time and they will feel homesick. Those who have learned to let others into their lives and give of themselves will soon find those they can love and who will love back.

Secrets about the nature of God are more easily discovered in the heart than in the head. Look for God through the good you feel and experience. If you go contrary to God and what the Creator represents your whole basis of belief will flicker and grow dimmer until it is all but undetectable. But practice being your best and your understanding of God will increase. Try to live as God intended humans to act toward each other, and you will find God.

Lemurian Tradition Verified By Discovery!

Men occasionally stumble over the truth,
but most of them pick themselves up and hurry
off as if nothing had happened.

– Winston Churchill

STUDY REVISES TIMELINE ON ARRIVAL OF HUMANS, blared the headline on page one of *The San Diego Union-Tribune* of April 26, 2017. We knew it would happen! So it's great to have Lemurian tradition verified by scientific proof that people actually lived on a continent where the Pacific Ocean lies now!

Understandably, the scientific community is not quite ready to make that quantum leap from the evidence recently reported in the news. They have to take things a careful step at a time, we know. But as a start, at least some are willing to say that a recent discovery in San Diego pushes back their estimates of when early man first showed up on the American continent by many thousands of years.

In case you missed it, all the excitement is about mastodon bones found at a construction site during freeway expansion here in San Diego. The bones were broken in a way that early humans used to get to the nutritious marrow, and then were made into useful tools. Surprisingly, this discovery happened 25 years ago, but only now have tests of uranium decay in the bones dated the site to 130,000 years ago – much before the 14,000 year estimate generally believed to be the earliest humans had been present on the American continent.

Those who have studied the Lemurian Philosophy, or taken a careful look at the Map of Mu, or Lemuria, the Fellowship has made available to the public, realize that the ancient Lemurian continent included much of the western United States including California. So the present site of San Diego was part of the Rhu Hut Plains of Mu 130,000 years ago as well as 50,000 years later, closer to the time when the world's first civilization got its start on those rolling plains.

Until this fact is more generally accepted, the mastodon bones, which show evidence of damage by human tools, will seem to indicate that early humans lived on, or at least visited, North America all those millennia ago. (The tribal chairman of the Sycuan Band of the Kumeyaay Nation said, "It's an exciting surprise and definitely does fit in line with the traditional creation story of the Kumeyaay people.")

But the question may well arise, how did those very primitive people manage to get here? It has long been assumed that the North American continent looked then as it does now, and the earliest people came from Asia, across a land bridge believed to have existed between what is now Siberia and Alaska. But as we know from Lemurian Philosophy, until the sinking of Mu, much of our present North America was mud flats. So rather than having to cross a trackless ocean or trek thousands of miles over frozen land bridges, these ancient hunters could simply have killed and dined on their shaggy prey on the eastern edge of their own homeland – Lemuria!

Daniel Fisher, a professor of paleontology, said "This is San Diego's chance to contribute to the knowledge of human history." We can hope the researchers will be inspired to probe beyond the appearance of their find, to the reality of the great continent that was home to the first and greatest civilization on this planet.

PERSONAL DEVELOPMENT

CHANGE YOUR MIND, CHANGE YOUR LIFE

The greatest discovery of any generation is that human beings can alter their lives by altering the attitudes of their minds.

– Albert Schweitzer

What could you accomplish if you had the Midas touch of Warren Buffet, the selflessness of Mother Teresa, the entrepreneurial genius of Bill Gates, the dedication to a cause of Nelson Mandela? If you could change your mind to think like any of these people, have their single pointedness of purpose, self-discipline, and drive, you could gradually become more like any of them.

When you can *change your mind* — not in the usual sense of reversing a decision, but fundamentally change your thinking — you change yourself and ultimately, your environment. We hear of people doing this in dramatic ways, like the former gang member who is mentoring young boys and men in his old neighborhood; the woman who was homeless, pregnant, and addicted at sixteen, now inspirationally helping girls at risk.

Paul the Apostle is probably one of the best known of those who have radically turned their lives around. Until his unforgettable religious conversion on the road to Damascus, Paul was a feared scourge of Christians who admitted that he "violently persecuted" this new religion. Yet, after he became convinced that Christ was really the long-promised Messiah, there was nothing he wouldn't do to help advance the Christian movement.

Few of us have the unusual devotion, the humility to admit we are on the wrong track, or the courage to completely change the course of our lives that Paul displayed. At least we probably *think* we lack these virtues, especially if we've never been in a situation where they were needed. But most of us have *some* devotion, courage, and humility. We can build on these beginnings and strengthen them. So why don't we?

You know the answer to that. Changing ourselves is hard. Anyone who has quit smoking, alcohol, or drugs knows this. For most of us, it takes many tries, a lot of talking to ourselves, and some agonizing effort, and even then we may relapse a few or many times before we finally make this profound turnaround in our lives. Often, there's a catalyst, like discovering you are pre-diabetic, before you can get serious about losing weight. In some fundamental way, we have to be deeply committed to changing ourselves to change our habits. But once we are, there are many boosts and supports to help us, much like having a personal trainer for weight loss.

This is where the Lemurian Philosophy comes in. If we have good reasons for changing our minds, the Philosophy can help us do it. When we understand the laws governing all life and human interaction and start working *with* these eternal principles instead of against them, our problems begin working out. Not all at once, but gradually. Most of us won't face the dramatic and momentous changes Paul or the other Disciples were called on to make. The changes we need to and can make are more modest, but potentially just as significant to us and those around us in our lives and environments.

Steadily, as we keep moving toward the good, the right, and the true, we experience in greater and greater measure

that more abundant life Christ promised all of us so long
ago.

The Sun Rises on a New World

There's a book most Lemurians have read countless times and many of us return to each year. It's *The Sun Rises,* a sacred guide we turn to for inspiration and practical answers. You might call it our Sourcebook. It's the true story of how the first civilization on this planet came together and woven into its pages is the recipe of basic rules on how to create the next great society, when the sun rises on a new world.

Within this captivating story of the long-ago characters who began the first cooperative endeavor on earth can be found early pearls of wisdom that were later strung together into lessons comprising the Lemurian Philosophy.

Have you ever heard or read a story that moved you deeply and touched a resonating chord within you? One that rang so true that you knew beyond a shadow of a doubt that the words came from divine authority and you felt enveloped in truth guided only by loving justice for all? And that within its spell, you are safe and at peace with all about you? This is how I feel when I read one of my favorite chapters, *Rhu and Hut Visit the Elders.*

When you read it, you may feel that way too. Your heart may be filled with hope, enthusiasm and inspiration for the world. You may say to yourself, "I am in full agreement with the wisdom I have just read. It's beautiful, and it would be the answer to the innermost prayer of every good person on earth. Who could disagree?"

But then, the old and deeply ingrained habit of negative thoughts and doubts may reassert itself and you sigh that the world is a mess, it seems it always has been and isn't getting any better. "Most everyone would agree it is in need of real serious change, and I would gladly follow the plan revealed in *The Sun Rises,* but what about others? I can't see them changing," you may protest.

But I reply that, if you feel the world is out of control, that there is no way out and the future is bleak, doesn't it seem obvious that continuing to do what comes naturally to most won't bring us the happiness we all seek? So, change we must, and change is possible if we start giving good thought to all we say and do, understanding that change won't happen overnight. It takes courage to go against the majority, too. But we can. If each of us does our part, we can.

Seventy-eight thousand years ago, a small group of rough-hewn people, some of them hereditary enemies, joined together and begin what eventually became the greatest civilization the world has yet known. Admittedly, they had much help from more highly developed people. But they did it. And so can we. A successful start has already been made, and all we need are people of courage, sincerity, and goodwill to help us move forward. We invite you to join us as the sun rises on a new world!

A Deeper Kind of Selfie

Know thyself.

– Socrates

Selfies are a fascinating phenomenon to those of us who grew up when people stood in awkward groups with stiff smiles on our faces if a camera was aimed at us. It's hard for some of us to understand why anyone would actually want themselves immortalized in this way. But it's intriguing to ask how this universal trend fits into life's purpose.

Cowboy philosopher Will Rogers said, "I always like to hear a man talk about himself because then I never hear anything but good." Most selfies are that way too – smiling faces, best profile, most flattering poses. Already that's changing, though, as people tire of seeing us at only our best. It may start downhill as we venture into the funny, the odd, the extreme, embarrassing, and bizarre selfies. At that point, the selfie may start to fade into history just as Polaroid instant photos did.

But another kind of selfie has been popular for centuries, even millennia, and probably always will be – autobiography. The best of these dig under the surface image, exploring the author's past, memories, influences and experiences, inner thoughts, concerns, and aspirations. Usually we go for this kind of "selfie" of the famous or the infamous, statesmen, sports greats, criminals, film stars or war heroes we want to know more about. But every human being has a story to tell, if only they would or could.

At its most engrossing, autobiography illuminates the writer's character, and even hints at the purpose of his existence. Benjamin Franklin's *Autobiography* reveals his faults and how he overcame them in remaking himself into one of the most famous and revered men of his time. These books inspire, guide, celebrate life and reveal how transforming it can be when you understand life's purpose and try to fulfill it.

Undoubtedly, the most honest and meaningful autobiographies are the ones each of us writes just for ourselves, and for God. With no concern about others' judgments or fear of being misunderstood, we can write what's in our hearts and see ourselves as none others see us. We can be completely honest about our motives, both good and not so good. We can affirm our strengths, admit our faults, and start to see how our strong points could help us improve the weaker ones.

In the constant effort to improve themselves, Lemurians write this deeper kind of selfie often, rating themselves against certain standards of character and conduct revealed in the Lemurian Philosophy. How tolerant am I; how courageous; how kind? What is my worst fault, and what did I do to overcome it this year? How am I helping others, and what more can I do for humanity next year?

This is the kind of selfie that counts. It's a picture of ourselves that actually gets better, year after year, and you just can't say that about your average selfie.

DISTANCE IS NO DETERRENT

Our life is what our thoughts make it.

– Marcus Aurelius

I was in Australia when I walked through the door of the old bookshop, a subtle but expectant feeling guiding me. What I discovered, and later more fully comprehended, changed my life forever.

I found a book with references to ancient Atlantis and other worlds. Reincarnation, too, and powerful references to atonement and evolvement. But the most significant reference mentioned the Lemurian Philosophy. And that introduced me to the Lemurian Fellowship, an association that's lasted 25 years.

I was far from home then. And though back in my native country, in a sense I am far from home now. The Fellowship and center of the Lemurian Philosophy is in Ramona, California, and here I am in England. But as I discovered half a lifetime ago, distance is no deterrent, and the Lemurian Philosophy works for me here, too.

You may wonder how that can be.

Watching the world news, I realize we are much the same. For the European struggling to come to terms with a distressed relationship, there's someone similar in Canada. A woman in Seattle wondering how to bring better morals to her children finds her counterpart in Africa facing the same dilemma.

I was struggling then with a change at work. I had just joined the local postal delivery office, a marked change for me that involved working outside in all weather. And I was dealing directly with the public, not to mention learning to adjust to some colorful character traits in my new colleagues!

I couldn't just pop round to talk all this over with my Fellowship teachers, so I thought about my predicament, organized my thoughts and wrote the Fellowship. When their helpful response came a short time later, I began to understand the advantages of the Lemurian training system. I'd had time to ponder the situation before their response came. My mind was calmer and I could appreciate more fully their sage advice.

My distance from the Fellowship, and the intervals between letters, proved helpful. I began to understand my role in events. I recognized the need to change my resistance and resentment to my new environment. I started working with the Fellowship's gentle, non-invasive advice and guidance. Like water wearing away the rock in its path, I started using Lemurian solutions to my problems. As I smoothed the rough spots around me, checking back for advice and assurance of being on the right track, positive changes gradually happened. I was growing and better understood many things.

I enjoyed my work more and appreciated more of the fine qualities in my colleagues. I was making more positive changes in myself, transmuting an unhappy working environment to a more satisfying and enjoyable one.

Today, most of my communication with the Fellowship is electronic instant messaging, and though it's quicker, I still welcome the intervals between letters. This gives me time to do my best so I may more fully profit from Fellowship correspondence.

I used to wonder, what if the Fellowship were in my hometown? I guess it would be easier to visit, but in terms of real and practical value, distance is no deterrent. The Masters can respond to our needs as quick as thought, and as their earthly channel, the Fellowship helps us wherever we may be.

Making Sense of Trouble

*In the long run, every man will pay the penalty for
his own misdeeds. The man who remembers this will
be angry with no one, indignant with no one, revile
no one, blame no one, offend no one, hate no one.*

– Epictetus

How good are you at making sense of trouble? When
life pulls the rug out from under you, can you reason out
why?

Sometime in mid-winter of 2014, my towel was stolen
off the hook at the YMCA. When I came out of the shower,
dripping wet, I found my towel gone and in its place a
worn and dirty look-alike. I was furious, and the fact that
the thief left a filthy towel in place of mine, one I wouldn't
use under any circumstance, only made matters worse.
When the emotion finally subsided and I had a chance to
reflect on it later that evening, I found myself remembering
a similar event that happened a half century earlier and
making sense of trouble.

I was nine or ten years old, spending a winter Saturday
at a nearby ski area. I was wearing a stylish ski hat that I
had inherited from one of my older brothers. It was a little
worn and a little dirty, but I felt very grown up wearing
it. While sitting at one of the tables in the main lodge, I
looked down and saw on the bench the very same hat as
the one I was wearing, only it was brand-spanking new,
clean and plush, probably just bought in the boutique shop,

or perhaps received as a Christmas present. It was the same color, the same size, identical in every way. It seemed too good an opportunity to pass up. I stole that hat and left my worn and dirty one in its place!

I suppose I made the switch as much to cover my tracks and give me time to get away with the goods, as I did out of a sense of decency, not wishing to leave its owner without a hat to wear on a cold winter day. My friend the towel thief probably felt much the same way. The temptation of a new and clean towel, small a thing as that may seem to be, probably triggered in him the same larcenous desire as that pristine ski hat had aroused in me some fifty years earlier.

My first reaction to the loss of my towel, of course, was one of indignation, of feeling wronged, yet it was inescapably clear that I had once wronged another in precisely the same manner as had now been done to me.

One major theme of the Lemurian Philosophy holds that we are not innocent bystanders in the events occurring in our lives. Putting forth the effort to sincerely study and apply the Philosophy can gradually raise our awareness to the point where we may correlate these events with our own thoughts and actions, making sense of trouble, bringing into our lives a greater sense of peace and understanding of ourselves and of others.

I had no claim to righteous indignation when my towel was taken. I am one of those people who believe that things happen for a reason. But were I not a student of the Lemurian Philosophy, I doubt whether I would ever have earned the opportunity to correspond these two events and gain valuable insight from the experience.

How to Slow Down and Start Living!

There is more to life than increasing its speed.

– Gandhi

Facebook! Twitter! Instagram! The news, the internet, TV, radio, or just ask Siri! How to slow down and start living is the urgent need of our time.

With so much information at our fingertips and in our faces, it's hard for people to get why they should investigate the Lemurian Philosophy, and even harder to slow down enough to actually try it. After all, if you're interested in Mu, there are countless books and websites offering every shade of interpretation of this term, from the sublime to the ridiculous. So why turn to the Lemurian Philosophy?

Many of us got into this study because we were interested in Lemuria, Atlantis, or ancient Egypt, and we've learned a lot. But that isn't why we decided to make this philosophy our way of life. That came from digging into the Lemurian information to understand its principles and appreciate its wisdom, then learning to use these with the Fellowship's help until we discovered for ourselves what they can do for us.

Take the Lemurian virtues. Everyone thinks they know what virtues are, and so what? Why bother to be kind when many people aren't, or even take advantage of your kindness? "I could be tolerant if I wanted to, but I don't see the point." Easy to say we could express a virtue if we wanted, but not so easy when you actually make the commitment to *do* it, no excuses. And you have to do it to find out what the point is.

If you're like most of us, once you're persuaded to improve your virtues, or at least try, you might decide to use patience for a day. You hold it in the back of your mind as you go to work. "Be patient" rings in your ears and you plan ahead for a couple of ways to *be* patient. But this takes a few tries, it turns out, because you keep running into people who need someone to set them straight, and others who clearly do not *deserve* your patience. But at last, you find the perfect conditions to wait twenty or thirty seconds longer before blowing your stack, and you feel a warm sense of accomplishment from using patience. That glow lasts about ten minutes, before some so-and-so does something to set you off again. But, no matter, that night you carefully document these events and, having conquered patience, set off the next day to master kindliness.

At that point, of course, you've made only the barest start at developing the power of patience, but it *was* a start. You realize just *reading* about patience, no matter how spiritual it makes you feel, doesn't confer the hard-won knowledge only *using* patience can bring. The patience to control ourselves and inspire others with confidence in us will never be ours until we pledge, "I really want to become a finer person, and I'm going to start with patience (or courage, or precision)."

There are eleven other virtues just as powerful and effective as patience to work on. But patience is a great one to start with, because it helps us slow the frenetic pace of our days so we can begin to recognize the wonderful possibilities, opportunities, sights, sounds and people around us. As much as anything, patience can help us learn how to slow down and start living, relax, and begin to truly enjoy the precious gift of life.

Junk Food for the Spirit

Have you ever thought about the effect negative thinking must have on the spiritual body? It's sort of like junk food for the spirit.

Finding a job after the Recession wasn't easy, but I finally found one that looked hopeful and I felt I could handle. And I loved the work, but felt out of place and inept, and started having stomach pains from self-generated stress. It would have been so easy at that point to climb aboard the train of negative thoughts we all ride to try to make ourselves feel better.

You know the routine: a supervisor seems a little sharp because we didn't understand a procedure, so we scheme how to get even or teach them a lesson. These negative thoughts seem to feel good, even fun for the moment. We get the same false sense of elation when we complain or rationalize some action and the adrenaline is pumping. This is junk food for the spirit. The immediate rush seems justified, but deep down we know too much of it will mean trouble.

This may take the edge off our frustration but hurts us in the long run. It ratchets up the tension, disrupts our health, often bringing headaches, stomach problems and more, yet it does nothing to change the cause of our anger, embarrassment, or self-pity.

But I know if we can catch ourselves soon enough and make the mental effort to keep our outlook positive, it helps us feel better too. Anger or worry can bring on headaches, but when the stress goes away the headache often does too. So I tried using positive thinking, every day, many times, to change my focus. It started with a little prayer of gratitude before I left home. At work, even though I felt anxious, I was determined to smile and be pleasant to the other employees and my boss. Gradually this worked its magic and I turned my thinking around.

It can be even more advantageous to nurture our spiritual bodies with positive thoughts and words as to feed our physical bodies with nutritious food. If we can make what we say and do to others encouraging, even healing, it helps make their days and ours go by harmoniously, peacefully and productively. If we're aware that negativity is like junk food for the spirit, we can consciously start to replace the space it's occupying with more helpful thoughts and words.

I still rely on positive thinking today, though it isn't easy to stay on the straight and narrow and takes time to change old habits. I still need to remind myself to think positively, so I always say that little prayer of thanks each morning. The rewards are sweet.

Next time those negative thoughts creep in, I highly recommend a nutritious snack of comforting, constructive thoughts. And every day offer some of those positives to your friends, co-workers and family. They'll really appreciate it, and you'll soon begin to discover a new, happier, and more confident you!

Lemurian Map Into Marriage

As I turned, nervous but purposefully to the person by my side, I knew a powerful and significant moment had arrived. I was about to commit to the culmination of a long-wished-for deep desire, fulfill a resolute goal, find the answer to a prayer. My Lemurian map into marriage had brought me to my wedding day!

What's the big deal? you might ask. People get married all the time, and for every one of them, it's special. What was so different for me? It's that I had a Lemurian map into marriage to bring me to this happy conclusion, and Lemurian tools to constructively pursue this personal happiness and desire.

It wasn't always this way. Not long ago I was rather despondent, devoid of confidence and unsure how to go forward. My previous relationships had irrevocably broken down. I felt anxious about my failures and wondered how I was ever going to move purposefully ahead. And it didn't happen overnight.

But the miracle of life is that it's an evolving process. Often the determining factor is just deciding *how* to forge ahead and then rediscovering that anchoring spring of exuberance and purpose that once was taken for granted. I was fortunate because here beside me was the Lemurian Philosophy to offer direction and the navigational tools I needed to place my feet firmly on that forward path.

I learned to change my thoughts and even my way of thinking, to believe in myself and gain confidence in projecting a positive aura of anticipated success.

With the Lemurian emphasis on quality and character development, I could discover the pleasing qualities and attributes I was looking for in another person if I did my part to earn this enlightenment. I knew I wanted to be with a kind person, so I went out of my way to be kind, and by working on this trait, attracted kindness into my life by the inevitable action of universal laws. Using these laws, I worked one by one on other characteristics important to me.

Another strong desire was someone to share leisure pursuits such as walking and cycling, so I joined a walking club to open up practical channels to help me along. I wanted someone with spiritual values and focused on attracting such a person into my life. It's a little like intensely wanting a certain sports car. After a while you spot the car at the turn of the road or sitting in a parking lot.

Over many months I moved ahead on an evolving and changing journey of thought and action, positively creating, developing myself to attract someone of similar attributes. How well I remember the day I met her as one of deep gratitude for being a Lemurian and having a Lemurian map into marriage. Now as I go forward, I feel blessed to continue working from my road map, evolving as I move into marriage and a life of beauty and purpose, one bright moment at a time.

STARTING LIFE OVER

*The battles that count aren't the ones for gold medals.
The struggles within yourself - the invisible,
inevitable battles inside all of us - that's where it's at.*

– Jesse Owens

When I grew up in Nigeria it was the custom for young parents who lived away from their tribe to send their children to the grandparents for training and schooling. So, at a very tender age I was sent to live with my grandmother, starting life over in a small rural village.

Traditional beliefs were strong, and sometimes ran wild. One quiet afternoon as we children played happily and old men rested lazily under large trees in the village square, gunfire suddenly erupted all around us. Men with sharp machetes shouted that ghosts were in the village, and all hell was let loose. People ran screaming in all directions as the terrified women herded the children to their homes. Fortunately, there was no loss of life or limb on that occasion. It ended well but made for an uncertain environment from day to day.

The mission school near the village was a pleasant oasis in this highly unpredictable environment. We loved the Bible stories and injunctions we were taught, but they did little to allay the fears that seemed a natural part of growing up. I had many unanswered questions, and sometimes held up a religious class with my questions about life. The answers didn't satisfy me, and nothing changed much until my junior year, when I became dangerously ill.

Two years in the hospital were painful, difficult, and lonely, culminating in heart surgery. Although I survived, I lost the ability to speak, write, and walk. Struggling to relearn these abilities was much harder because I completely lost my confidence.

Having to relearn everything I had already mastered as a child was so much harder this time. I was really starting life over now. I could no longer write with my right hand but had to start all over again with my left. Eventually I recovered and went back to complete high school.

After this inexplicable experience, I struggled with even more urgent questions about life and why my illness occurred. If there was ever a person searching for answers, it was I.

Around that time, I learned about the Lemurian Philosophy, and while at a university in the U.S. became a Lemurian student and finally began to find answers to my troubling questions about life. They were clear, unambiguous, logical, and intensely practical. By applying principles the Philosophy teaches, I learned much more and began to deduce many answers for myself, and this education continues today.

My self-confidence began to return. I completed my education and returned to my homeland as an engineer, feeling reborn. My accomplishments mean so much more to me because of all I have been through, and I will always be grateful to those wise and kindly Great Ones who help us in our times of extreme need and watch over us through the surprising twists and turns of our ongoing, sometimes even helping us through starting life over to fulfill the purpose of our lives.

Happiness and Well-Being

Looking for More in Life

*He who wishes to know the road through the
mountains must ask those who have trodden it.*

– Chinese Saying

Among the many genuinely interested or simply curious people who come up the Lemurian Fellowship's driveway to talk with us are many who are looking for more in life. We try to help them discover whether the Lemurian Philosophy resonates with what they trust and believe in and offers new vistas they want to explore.

While many have heard of Lemuria, their ideas about it and the truths that made it great are all over the map. So we are always happy to explain the Fellowship's role as a School with the sacred responsibility of teaching Lemurian Philosophy and training serious aspirants who are looking for more in life how to use these ancient principles to enhance their lives and help others in harmony with universal law.

We've seen a dramatic increase in people's general information about Lemuria in the last 80 years, and more and more often, we are hearing from those who seem powerfully drawn to what they feel or believe is here, yet strangely hesitant to give the Lemurian Philosophy a try. Because this paradox is increasingly common, we've thought about it. And we think we know why.

Unless we have unusual control over our environments, all of us live with chronic information overload. The media, our computers, our smart phones not only offer us almost infinite resources, trivial and profound, but they contact us, remind us, tempt us and pursue us through our days and ding away into the once peaceful hours of the night. We have so much information at our fingertips, eyes and ears, there's not enough time to assimilate it, organize it, or think much about it. For those who battle with this incessant intrusion into their thoughts, there seems no chance for anything else, not to mention the ever-present concern for privacy and not wanting to be hounded by emails or other follow-ups after finding answers to our questions.

Maybe because there seems no time for concentration or deeper thought, it somehow seems like information itself must be enough. If you have enough *information* about the wisdom of the ancient Lemurians, isn't this good? It's like the fine quotes shared on Facebook. Many hold universal truths. But they flit into and out of our minds so quickly, replaced each day with the next wise and interesting quotation, do we really give them time to take root and mean something?

The problem is, information is only a collection of facts, and until we actually *prove* those facts in our experience, we don't even know if they are true. Fellowship students convert the Lemurian *information* into *knowledge* by applying it in their lives. They use the Law of Precipitation to bring desired things and conditions into their lives. The Law of Compensation helps them eliminate debt and build prosperity by making *spiritual* changes in their thinking and living. Compassionate teachers help them do this efficiently and in harmony with other universal laws that also affect everything we do and all that happens to us.

So for all who knock on the Fellowship's door, enjoy a few minutes' conversation and the peaceful beauty of this location, and take away our web address or brochure, we look forward to the time when you feel the urge to investigate further and discover all that the Lemurian Masters would so gladly offer you through their earthly channel, the Lemurian Fellowship.

LIVING THE UNIVERSAL DREAM

*Our environment is the exact material
arrangement of our thinking.*

– Lemurian Philosophy

For over two centuries, people have been making their way to America, hoping for a better life and believing they could find it here. And whether or not they aspire to the American Dream, people everywhere long for something better, and to be living the Universal Dream.

The yearning for happiness and security in beautiful surroundings is universal. But like a child reaching for the moon, what people reach for seems to elude their grasp. Uncertainty about what we want and how to get it makes it impossible to attain.

Most of us *think* we know what we're aiming for. The poor believe if they had enough money, they would be happy. But the wealthy still feel dissatisfied and try to fill the void with extravagant pleasures. The unwell are sure better health is the answer. But with each dream fulfilled, the unknown and seemingly unattainable still beckon us toward something more.

This longing causes many to turn to Truth, hoping a better understanding of God, the universe, and the unknown will bring meaning to life. When they learn of the Lemurian Masters, who have studied the histories of every human civilization and have evolved a Plan for an ideal society with none of the flaws of our present ones, they want to be part of it.

In building this new civilization, we have thousands of years of experience using our hands and minds to create the entrancing wonders we have today and will have tomorrow. But we have a serious handicap – thousands of years of wrong thinking, destructive ideas and bad habits. We have learned to our sorrow and almost to the point of self-destruction, how to cooperate *destructively*. Before we can make real progress, we must *un*learn and overcome these negative thinking habits.

It is a universal law that we can have and keep only what we ourselves have earned. As long as we keep trying to get something for nothing and place ourselves above the good of others, we will be paying off karmic debts that lead to war and misery, poverty and disease. But as we sincerely work to overcome wrong thoughts and actions, we begin to improve our environment and master ourselves. Thoughts can build all that is good and true and beautiful, just as they have so long been used to tear it down.

To create a beautiful environment, we must first build beauty in our thoughts. A wonderful power to create has been given us! And those who sincerely desire to help build the Kingdom of God are recognizing what's negative and destructive in their own hearts and minds and changing it into what's positive and constructive. Like the Phoenix, they are rising from the ashes of their old thinking. From their faces radiates the serenity of those who have found that peace which passeth all understanding. Their entire being reflects the power and confidence they're gaining. Each of them is establishing a personal New World, joining others who are doing the same, gradually expanding their more ideal life. They are living the Universal Dream.

Extremes or Moderation?

*Moderation is the silken string running
through the pearl chain of all virtues.*

– Joseph Hall

Today's keyword must be *EXTREME!* Extreme sports, politics, candy, drinks, flavors, electronics, escapes and more drown out the subtler tones like a rock concert makes it hard to hear life's normal sounds for a while. In all the noise there's little space for the gentler peace of *moderation* and *balance*. Do these terms seem boring *in the extreme* to you? Or do the quieter vibrations of moderation and balance resonate at some deep level as you search unconsciously for the serenity these qualities promise?

How would you rate your personal balance? Is your schedule hectic, filled with too much to do? Do you gulp down fast food because you're too busy or tired and just want to feel good, hoping those fries will do it? All of us crave exhilaration in meeting the day's events and complementary times of peaceful rest. But how can we experience that if our calendar alarm launches us full tilt through our waking hours?

Counterintuitive as it seems, things begin to settle into place if we can get off the merry-go-round long enough to slow down, be still, and listen. At first the hectic pulse of life outside your door may seem to make this impossible. Your mind races off in seven directions. You may feel extremely uncomfortable being alone with your own thoughts at first. But on the other side of that discomfort beckons a sense of tranquility and self-control well worth the effort. Are you strong enough to calm your unruly thoughts, turn off your phone, TV, or computer and explore the wonders of quiet reflection?

In these precious moments, can you talk with God about yourself, your life, your fears and your gratitude, and trust He is listening? And as they tell us to do on a flight, put your oxygen mask on first, so you can help others with theirs.

Why *make* that effort? Because, if the most important requisites for human spiritual advancement could be summed up in two words, they would be *moderation* and *balance.*

A fanatic can't be moderate because he closes his mind to everything that doesn't agree with his view. He refuses to consider any except his own which gets narrower and narrower until it becomes a rut. Fanaticism, prejudice and intolerance bring so much human misery. Moderation, open-mindedness, and tolerance lead inevitably to balance, understanding, and inclusion.

To make important progress as human beings, our lives must be lived in a way that equalizes spirituality, mentality, and materiality. As we move closer to that beautiful balance, real advancement comes within reach. You can prove this for yourself. Pick one place where you know you go overboard. Maybe when you talk about something you're deeply interested in, you over-embellish and say too much. You know how this affects you when you hear it. But how restful and interesting to listen to someone who is moderate in his voice and his words. Almost always, moderation is more convincing and reassuring than wild enthusiasm.

So start today to use moderation and balance in all you say and do. Consciously reach toward that peaceful, controlled outlook so characteristic of those like the Masters, who are really advanced, knowing the nearer we come to balance, the closer we are to earning a place in the better world of tomorrow, and the more we can help those around us.

Why not try it for a week? Let us know what happens. We would be most interested.

We Won't Lose Our Minds

So much that I've learned from the Lemurian Philosophy has become part of my daily living and thinking that I sometimes forget just how blessed I am to have this unique source of understanding and guidance. Sometimes, it's too easy to take the knowledge I've gained from my studies for granted, but then an experience comes along that brings its value into sharp focus. For instance, it's most reassuring to know that in spite of appearances, we won't lose our minds.

My father has dementia. On a good day, he gets confused. On a bad day, he thinks people are trying to kill him.

This is the same man who worked for 40 years as an electrical engineer, eventually becoming a recognized authority on the radar used in the F-16 fighter jet. His mind was razor sharp and I soon came to know that if he remembered something in a particular way, I could trust that he was right.

An especially fond childhood memory shows how his mind worked. One day we were at the ocean, standing at the water's edge watching tankers on the horizon move up and down the coast. I asked him how far it was to the horizon. I was expecting a simple answer like, "Oh, about four miles or so." Instead, I got something like: "Let's see…the curve of the earth is such and such. We're at sea level so we don't have to factor in any atmospheric distortion. Your eyes are about three feet above ground, and mine are about five and a half feet. So the angle is …

for you, and … for me." Then, based on these observations, he gave some very specific distances, such as 3.9 miles for me and 4.2 miles for him.

How different it is now! With his dementia, not only can my dad not remember what time dinner is, he can't figure out that if dinner is at 5:00 and it's 4:15, it will be another 45 minutes. Sometimes, he doesn't remember that he already ate. And yet, in the face of this experience, I'm confident that we won't lose our minds. I know my dad doesn't have much more time with us, and when he passes through transition, we will be sad. But I also know something very reassuring.

The Lemurian Philosophy explains that the brain is a physical organ, the mind a power that operates through the brain. We are assured that even though most people's bodies and brains break down as they near the end of this physical life, we won't lose our minds. My dad is just having an increasingly difficult time using this physical organ, his brain, to express himself. But when he does pass over to the unseen side, all the hard-earned intelligence, knowledge, and wisdom he has gained in this full and successful life will go with him. Nothing will be lost. He will be full and complete and ready for whatever great adventure lies ahead.

HAPPINESS SECRET REVEALED

What makes you happy? I had the happiness secret revealed to me the other day when an elderly gentleman in another state contacted me. He knew I repair old radios, and had one he wanted fixed but no one in his area would tackle it. It was one of the first commercial tube sets built and had been given to his grandmother at Christmas in 1921. We arranged for him to bring it to my shop the next weekend. Since it was a seven-hour trip for him, I wanted to be sure I was ready for him so I took time to gather together all the radio parts I thought I might need.

When he arrived, I laid out the radio and hooked it up using the original instructions that came with it. The tube in it was bad, but I had set a replacement aside just in case. So I put it in. With all the wires for antenna, ground, power supply and headphones coming out of it, the radio looked like it was on life support! And then the moment of truth arrived when I fired it up. I was able to pick up a faint station right away through the headphones and with some tuning got it coming in nice and strong.

I handed the headphones to my customer and watched his face light up when he heard it playing. I had the feeling this must have been the reaction to first hearing radio back in the 1920s. He had never heard it play and it was the one keepsake he had to remind him of his grandmother. When he was a child she had told him about first listening to it. He was delighted to be able to listen to the same radio his grandmother had used.

It really brightened my day to see the wonder and amazement on his face at something so commonplace today — listening to a radio. His happiness in hearing this radio for the first time matched mine in being able to restore a historical bit of radio history to its original use for its owner! By thinking about him and taking the time to have everything I might need available, I was able to bring a little bit of wonder to another individual. And seeing his face light up brought me a deep sense of joy.

I know you've experienced something similar. Did you ever surprise someone with a gift they weren't expecting? The look on their face as they take in what you've done for them is worth all the trouble. And we all know people who can put a smile on your face by telling you a lame joke or finding the humor in some serious situation. They can cheer you up just by being around. They have had the happiness secret revealed to them and chances are, they're very happy people.

So is the happiness secret revealed. You can count on being happy if you make someone else happy!

Safe Harbor
in a Turbulent World

As each day brings us scenes of sectarian conflict and heart-wrenching misery, I wish I could share what I've learned with these poor, afflicted people and help them find a safe harbor.

My daughters and their families are Catholic, my son Jewish, his wife, Buddhist. My sisters are Unitarian, one brother follows the Tao and another ranges through many schools of thought. My in-laws include Spanish and Irish Catholics, Conservative and Reformed Jews. All are good, moral people. I can see that each of their beliefs has its place and purpose for them, and helps them navigate life.

But different beliefs can separate people, creating dissension and discord.

When my husband and I agreed to divorce, I found that my church would accept me only if I denied my marriage through annulment, which would be very expensive and make my children's births legally ambiguous. I told my father I no longer felt our church was for me. He was furious. He tried to dissuade me, not from the divorce, which was needed, but from leaving my church. When I wouldn't comply with his wishes, he sent me away, telling me never to come back to his home.

I did move away, and met the man who would become my second husband. Then his parents tried to dissuade him from marrying me because I was not of his faith! But he accepted me and we made our marriage work. We raised our son in the Jewish tradition, and I investigated many beliefs, looking for a safe harbor. I always loved Christ's message but was surprised how differently it was interpreted by divergent groups.

Then I got a job working for a boss who had a cheerful and kind way of running things – a breath of fresh air in the working world. I wondered what made him tick. One day I asked him about a beautiful wooden box on his desk. He said it had been hand crafted by fellow students at the school where he studied the Lemurian Teachings, derived from an ancient civilization on a continent that had once existed in the Pacific Ocean.

I had heard of the "lost continent of Mu," and was intrigued. When I found the Lemurian Fellowship was a distance-learning school, so you could study at home wherever you lived, it didn't take me long to write. I wanted the calm, cheerful faith my boss had!

I learned that the Lemurian Philosophy is based on Christ's teachings and it was presented in a straightforward, inclusive way. As I read the lessons and corresponded with the teachers, the history of the world and how things came to be as they are, made more and more sense. How each belief system began was revealed, along with the need for everyone to understand and use basic virtues and universal laws to create a better and happier life. We aren't really so different from each other, after all.

My years as a Lemurian student working to understand and apply tolerance, so difficult to practice consistently, have enabled me to more calmly accept decisions my beloved family members have made, as their own and right for them. If this simple thing could be done by everyone, all could find this safe harbor and how much closer to harmony the world could be!

Search for Happiness

So universal is the search for happiness that those who wrote the Constitution of the United States of America wanted to guarantee us the right to pursue it.

Ever since we humans first grew conscious of our individual identities, we have felt this driving urge to seek an elusive something we call *happiness.* For the earliest people, satisfying personal needs seemed to offer it. But even with shelter and a full belly, the desire persisted. The companionship of others brings a fleeting glimpse of happiness, but we can't hold onto it. We try amusements that trick the senses into feeling we have found happiness. We try various escapes, reaching momentary highs at the cost of our health, wealth, and well-being. But these lose their appeal, and we resume our eternal quest.

We still feel this unfulfilled longing, and gradually realize we don't seem to have the power to attain happiness. Somehow, we have missed the key. Admitting we are *not* self-sufficient, we seek the help always provided for the sincere and humble. As Christ encouraged us, "Seek and ye shall find. Knock and it shall be opened unto you."

We begin to think – really *think* – leading us to investigate higher truths. The constant and insistent search for happiness has been implanted within our innermost being, and this desire in the earliest human beings was our motivation to start moving toward the ultimate goal of all human existence – happiness.

Our time on earth is a means to an end, for the ultimate goal *is* happiness. Otherwise, heaven, either the Kingdom of God here on earth or the final attainment in a celestial realm, will be impossible. Heaven means a place of perfect happiness where all will have learned to control themselves and their environment, molding them into the ideal the innermost self has been so eternally seeking. There is no reason we shouldn't search for happiness here and now, even though it won't be perfect until we are at one with God.

Our *experiences* are the stepping-stones to the wisdom and understanding essential to happiness, and it is possible to enjoy some of this as we pass through these experiences, if we remember they are essential to attaining true soul growth. But we make many experiences bitter because we fail to abide by God's simple rules.

Essential to true happiness is banishing fear and worry. And since fear is a most powerful emotion, we must avoid it if we are to reach our goal. Can you picture serenity in an atmosphere of fear – of illness, of losing our job, of being in debt, of something bad happening? *Having* such fears is the surest way to bring them into our lives. Every time we feel this emotion, we may know we are not using some cosmic law, sacrificing happiness because of our ignorance.

What's the cure? When you want to bring something into your life, concentrate on it. If you don't want to be the victim of fear, cease to give it power by deliberately and positively using your God-given *will power* to *think of something else!* Something you really *want* in your life and environment. If your mind reverts to fear, *train* your mind, using the techniques described in the Lemurian lessons. Otherwise, fear will dominate and you will never fulfill the search for happiness.

Precipitation Finds a Life Partner

Away from home and on my own in college I seemed to feel each experience more intensely since the choices were mine alone. Dating brought its excitement as well as heartaches, but gradually I reached a point of discouragement as I realized the guys I was dating weren't ones I could visualize a future with.

As a Lemurian, I knew how to use the Law of Precipitation to bring desired conditions into my life. But could I find a life partner with precipitation?

There are six steps of the precipitation process, each vital to success. The first and most important is intense desire, and that I certainly had. And an unwavering desire made it easier to do whatever was needed to fulfill the other steps.

The second step is visualizing the desired object, so that was my next job. I started a journal of the qualities in friends and family members that I wanted in a spouse. It was hard to pinpoint these at first, but in time I came up with quite a specific list. He would need to be thoughtful, generous, intelligent, hard-working, open-minded . . . and as the list came together, I started feeling optimistic about meeting someone!

Every romantic relationship led me back to my list to see if I had encountered traits to add or delete, knowing I was on a path leading me somewhere wonderful.

The other four steps of precipitation were also on my mind and carefully carried out during these interesting weeks and months.

I knew I would have the help of the Masters who watch over us and extend their aid when we have done our best, and I tried to compensate them by helping others around me. All these things, I knew, were part of the journey toward the important and life-changing goal I was trying to reach. And I knew it would work out for my greatest good as long as I was doing my part.

One day I agreed to a blind date that left me intrigued. A few dates in, it was clear I had found someone special who possessed traits most important to me, and I realized I was falling in love. We married a year later.

I often think about my list and all the time I spent carefully choosing the characteristics and visualizing my life with this very special person, and actively seeking him. By using what the Lemurian Philosophy taught me, and finding a life partner with precipitation, I changed frustration into optimism and created the positive experience I most desired in my life.

PATIENCE PATH TO PEACE

The Patience path to peace is one approach taught in the Lemurian Philosophy to create a more tranquil life. To those who have not walked this path, it may appear simple: all you have to do is not react to the things that would otherwise frustrate and irritate. Not so! Patience is not passiveness. It requires unusual self-control and is an essential step toward self-mastery.

Here are two stories from today's Lemurians showing how they are using patience to gain conscious control over their lives and affairs:

* * *

In the Lemurian Philosophy we have a time-honored explanation of the Virtue Patience from one of the Elder Brothers who guide our Work:

He whose rice crop has failed and whose children know want, yet can listen with tolerant understanding to him who has a broken fingernail, knows patience.

As with other statements in the Lemurian Philosophy, I recognized this one as important and even memorized it, but I had no real feeling for its meaning or how such a thing could even be accomplished, until a day when I had a medical appointment.

The weather was frigid, so I decided to take the bus instead of walking as usual. The bus was running very late and I started to worry that I might not make my appointment on time. When at last it came and I got on, I was totally wrapped up in my own concerns. The people getting on and off the bus were no more than impediments holding me back as I counted the minutes to my appointment time.

Recognizing this self-absorbed intolerance for what it was, I decided to make the Lemurian effort to set myself completely aside and focus on those other riders. What were their needs? What were they like? This shift of focus had the welcome effect of eliminating all sense of worry and brought back a measure of calm, further helping me tune into the people and activities around me.

I was amazed at how well this worked and the memory of it stayed with me for days. I felt I had a small but valuable success with patience and began to think about setting myself aside and thinking of others as a potential cure for many ills. I went back to the lesson that teaches how to develop patience, and after reading the quotation from the Elder Brother, I wrote in the margin: "He set aside self-interest to think of others before himself."

* * *

Before I became a Lemurian, I had memorized a Bible verse, but never had a thought about what it meant:

"Let patience have her perfect work, that ye may be perfect and entire," (James 1:4)

After working on the Lemurian virtues for many years, now I feel I can probably delve into that verse for the rest of my life and get deeper meanings every time I do. What a wonderful thing to know that when we do develop patience to the nth degree, we will be perfect and entire, wanting nothing. I am overwhelmed with the power in that verse and determined to keep it as my goal.

I had been enjoying picking my grandkids up at school one day a week for my daughter, but then her work hours changed and now she is delivering the kids to me at 6:30

and I take them to school every morning. Last week it was pouring rain and I had three and a half hours in the car every day. I had such patience, never once feeling stressed or sorry for myself and enjoyed the time with the kids. Actually, got them talking about something other than video games a few times! It was so easy to practice patience and so much more fun than exploding with impatience.

When I picked up my grandson at school the other day, I was a little early, and he was ten minutes late. It seemed longer, and I was getting worried . . . not really impatient, but worried that we hadn't understood each other. He didn't have his phone so I couldn't text him. When he finally came, I didn't show impatience at all but merely said, "Why so late?" He said his binder had been stolen the day before and the teacher was giving him the work that was stolen so he could redo it. I was so grateful I hadn't shown any impatience with that dear boy!

Patience even has so much to do with grief! I said goodbye to my husband very recently and I have found that expecting to get over someone you have spent 60 years with, in a few days or months, or years, or ever, is not understanding patience and letting it have its perfect work.

Dr. Stelle wrote: "When all else has failed, try patience. It will save you many heartaches. It will solve an unbelievable number of your hardest problems, and most of the time, is actually the shortest path to success. It will bring into your environment a peace that can be experienced in no other way."

RECEIVING AND GIVING

TRUE FRIENDS RESCUE

Loving kindness is greater than laws,
and the charities of life are more than all ceremonies.

– The Talmud

A Thanksgiving Story

In our world now, so many are facing devastating floods, storms, fires and worse, and at times like these, seeing the good-hearted love and help of strangers and friends alike is unforgettable.

We had such an experience recently. We were away from the Fellowship barely two hours that Saturday night, but coming back, my wife and I found water pouring out the front door, half an inch covering the hall and kitchen tile, and a fire hose blast of hot water from the bathroom. Wading in there revealed a steamy Niagara Falls pouring from the sink cabinet. Turning an angle stop had no effect so I sprinted outside and shut off the water supply. Seeing water dripping from the ceiling, I prayed the sprinkler system hadn't burst, and in the first good news of the evening, we found this was only condensation from the steamy air.

As our true friends rescue team arrived to help mop up the tile floors, we turned our attention to the water seeping under the carpets and across the rooms. We called an emergency flood service and plumber, only half expecting either would respond at 8:00 Saturday night. But what a blessing! Both came within an hour. The plumbing fix was simple – a ruptured angle stop feed line. Unfortunately, water soaking under carpets had already reached the furniture and walls and would soon wick up into the drywall. Carpets would have to come up and be dried out and, worst case scenario, we might have to remove and replace some drywall.

Meanwhile, our true friends rescue team had somehow spread the word, converged, and gone to work. They finished mopping and started moving things off wet carpets and out of the house. It wasn't just picking up wet furniture – it was removing *everything,* even from the walls, so the vacuum and driers could work. More friends arrived from Gateway to help. We had just moved everything to the patio when, as if to test our resolve, it started raining and blowing onto the patio! We hurried to cover the exposed furniture and boxes with plastic and went to bed, exhausted.

Next morning, Sunday, should have been a day of rest for those who work six days a week, but with dehumidifiers blasting hot air constantly throughout the house our true friends were back early to help move furniture and boxes from the patio to another building, safe from weather and mice during the week-long drying-out.

During that week there were countless examples of the quiet, thoughtful helpfulness we associate with Lemurians, but seldom need to depend on this much. They took time from their own work to shoulder our duties, stayed with us as long as we needed help through the week of repairing and repainting walls. It felt like a pioneer barn-raising when neighbors came from miles around to help with a job too much for one family.

One brought us a care package of useful things like a flashlight when we couldn't find ours and snacks when we couldn't get to ours. No complaint about the extra workload was heard, though we know each of them has a very full schedule every day. Everyone seemed to take it all in stride.

We feel a deep and timeless spiritual connection to these selfless, reliable true friends of longstanding, not only in this life but who we are sure have worked with us other lives too. Our dual purpose of perfecting ourselves and helping others benefit from the Lemurian way of life never seemed more essential, or more satisfying, than it has since that difficult but very heartwarming night.

How to Help Humanity

Give a man a fish, you feed him for a day.
Teach a man to fish, you feed him for a lifetime.

Do you ever wonder how to help humanity in genuinely lasting and effective ways? How do you try to help the hungry, homeless, depressed, those struggling with problems or otherwise in need who seem deserving of your caring and support?

Through donations, many kind and generous people make a positive difference. But giving to even a fraction of the good causes around the world would leave most of us broke and needing help ourselves. And giving money is like giving a man the proverbial fish. It may help as long as the money holds out, but then he's back where he was.

Then there are those unintended consequences. If we give a homeless person a few dollars, we don't really know if this will feed his family, as his sign says, or buy him drugs or alcohol, leaving him weaker and even less able to fend for himself.

Habitat for Humanity and other programs approach the problem more directly, raising homes and prospects for many. Commendable and very satisfying, but not yet teaching a man to fish, or solving his difficulties. How will the recipient furnish this new home and maintain it?

Even personal help is complicated. We think we know just what will help a troubled friend, so we offer advice.

But without knowing *why* he hit this particular snag, or the full nature of the trouble, our advice could easily make a bad situation worse.

We could just *listen*. This may have more chance of helping than any idea so far, because when he can talk out a problem with a trusted friend or even a sympathetic stranger, often he begins to see how he could tackle it. If this gives him a fresh start he pursues with new enthusiasm, we may really have made a difference.

But even this falls short of teaching him to fish. Because even if he succeeds, where will he turn for support when the next trouble comes along? How can we help people learn to take control of their lives, manage their challenges in ways most beneficial for them and others? In the Teachings of the Masters, we discover many little-known factors that determine how truly effective our efforts to help can be.

The Lemurian manual for superlative living explains universal laws and how they apply to all of us. It shows how to use them to enhance our circumstances, create our desires, overcome personal weaknesses, and become stronger, better people. As we do this we make ourselves part of the better world so urgently needed now.

Thousands of people taking the Lemurian training have improved their marriages, work and family ties and friendships; tracked down better jobs; worked out of debt; overcome hindering challenges; become happier by learning how to help humanity and serve God. *They're finding a feeling of purpose, of calm and of peace.*

So we think the best way to help anyone with just about any need, want, or trouble, is to introduce him to the Lemurian Philosophy. And then cheer him on!

BLAST OF UNDERSTANDING BRINGS FAITH

All I have seen makes me trust in all I have not seen.

– Emerson

Sometimes, disturbing events can shake our faith in what we believe. And faith has always been a challenge for more or less balanced people seeking a spiritual path. Their high ideals draw them toward it, yet their practical caution raises doubts. We know that understanding brings faith, and for those who do find the path that's right for them, there are always reassurances along the way, just as there are warning signs for those on a false trail.

Students of the Lemurian Philosophy have their struggles with faith too. Sometimes the proofs we need come in dramatic ways, as they did in this early experience.

In the 1940s there was much hard physical work at the Lemurian Fellowship's Ramona site. Three buildings had been constructed by hand using concrete blocks the staff and students produced themselves, one by one. At the site of the fourth building, some blasting was needed to clear the large boulders they encountered.

In those days, you simply went to the hardware store and bought dynamite. One of the Fellowship staff, Carl, had considerable experience with blasting. He and a helper set and lit a charge, then moved away a safe distance. When it failed to detonate within what they thought was a reasonable time, they came forward to investigate. It exploded, injuring both of them, Carl more seriously.

Some Fellowship students, young in understanding, believed this should not have happened if the Fellowship was protected by the Masters, and asked Dr. Stelle about this. Here is his reply.

"I have done a great deal of thinking about the dynamite incident, but he who most seriously injured himself offered the best explanation, to which I attach a great deal of importance. Now, as to some reason for the happening, aside from the carelessness:

"There are many who often question whether there are Masters, whether the Great Work is all it seems to be, if it is directly under Their supervision, and as to the authenticity of the Work. Carl said he had often been prey to these very things and that, while his reason told him everything was exactly as we say it is, still there was in his mind, at times, lingering doubt based on previous experiences with different occult organizations.

"Doubts like these die hard, but understanding brings faith, and having had plenty of experience with dynamite, Carl realized something of what had transpired. After the incident, someone said they wondered why Carl was willing to keep working here when this had happened, and whether he didn't feel that the Work could not be under the Masters' guidance and protection.

"Carl said his reaction had been exactly the opposite. With his knowledge of the power of dynamite, he realized that nothing but the intervention of some high source could possibly have prevented his and the other worker's being blown to bits. Plus they have come through practically without suffering, and their recovery has been so marvelously rapid, there could no longer be any question in his mind.

"Frankly, if the entire experience did nothing more than satisfy Carl with the authenticity of this Work, it would have been worth ten times the delay and inconvenience involved, for after all, if he who was most seriously injured so regards it, who are we to attach any less importance to it?"

Spiritual Help in a Firestorm

One of the most difficult experiences of my life was being caught in a fierce wildfire. When my husband and I saw smoke in the distance with strong dry desert winds behind it, we knew a fire was headed our way. But no fire planes were taking off from the nearby airport, due to the strong winds.

Sometimes Lemurian students expect that we will get spiritual help to spare us from such disasters because we are trying to live by the Lemurian Teachings and we believe in God and the Masters. Some are disappointed to find that disasters touch many of our lives. But we were helped in a most ingenious way.

That night we got a reverse 911 call telling us to evacuate, but before we knew it the fire was upon us. We raced to a large shop on open, well-cleared land with fire hoses previously set up at the ready. As the dry hot winds fed the flames surrounding our property, the noise was unnerving. And it was hard to know which way the fire would go with the winds so erratic.

Yet, each time I prayed, "please may the winds die down so our town will be spared and all who live in it," the winds seemed to kick up. It was almost like being mocked.

I felt like a spiritual failure, I was so inept at prayers God hears.

As we stood there helplessly watching the flames burning around us on all sides, the scorching wind and fire roared like a wild animal. But inside that seeming chaos was also a quietness – a sense of something so much bigger than we are. I felt the only thing solid is God. And the only thing strong enough to save us was God. Would I deny God by not believing all would be as it should be?

Gradually, with amazement and relief, I realized that because the winds *were* blowing so fiercely, the fire raced through our property so fast it barely touched most of our buildings long enough to set them alight. It burned right up to the buildings but left most of them intact!

Only *because* the winds stayed so strong were we spared from destruction! Had God and the Masters granted my prayer and slowed the winds, we might have lost everything. I'd wanted God to do what I felt was best, not what He knew was best! I guess it's natural to think this way in a life-threatening situation. But it's funny to look back on this puzzled human being standing there with her hands on her hips wondering why, when she prays, the winds don't instantly die down – and deciding she must be spiritually inadequate!

We came through it so well that while hundreds of acres around us were nothing but charred earth and rocks, our several buildings remained mostly intact, a small oasis of green. Viewing this from the top of one of our hills, it was proof that in times of greatest danger, God always extends the assistance we need. God hears my prayers. It was almost like hearing God say, "See, I was here. Thanks for offering to direct things, but I had it in hand."

Lemurian Advice About Advice

Advice is seldom welcome. Those who need it most like it least.

– Johnson

In his history of the Lemurian civilization, Dr. Stelle tells of Rhu, the greatest archer of that age, trying to help his brother make a more effective bow. But in the competitive spirit of brothers, Grut would rebel. In time, Grut became interested enough to actually *ask* Rhu about this. And *then* he followed his directions to the letter! This story highlights an important Lemurian principle about advice and a well-loved saying from those days,

Advice unasked for is much like salt. A little of it goes a long way. – Lithargos

Lemurians believe every adult has a divine right of self-determination, the right to accept help (advice) from others, or not. There's a delicate balance to be observed, and giving advice when it is neither asked nor wanted can be a serious intrusion into others' lives.

How do you feel about advice? Do people listen to your efforts to help, and do they seem to benefit from your words of wisdom? Turning this around, do you listen to and benefit from advice others direct your way?

Have you tried to correlate your giving and receiving of advice? If your hackles rise when anyone tries to suggest a tip or show you a better way of doing something, how does this affect your own efforts to advise others? If you think about advice from others as a pain in the neck, does this deter you from giving advice?

On the other hand, if you look for and find the good in the help people offer you, does this make you a wiser and more competent advisor?

Benjamin Franklin wrote:

Those who cannot be counseled, cannot be helped…there is nothing to be done but wait until experience comes forth to teach its lessons. We can give advice, but we cannot give conduct.

So while we have the right to disregard all help from others – the natural tendency of every two-year-old – we find it pretty slow going if we insist on meeting every experience entirely on our own without guidance or assistance. Yet, as the quotation admits, *experience* is the best teacher. An experienced swimmer can give us all the best pointers, but until we get in the water and try it, there's a lot we still have to learn for ourselves.

There's a problem with advice: to the receiver, it's only information, not experience. It may work for the person who tells us about it, like a health remedy Aunt Sheila swears by but doesn't do a thing for us. So we have reason to be skeptical about advice, and careful about offering it. We don't want to seem less intelligent or like we need advice, of course. But don't you admire people who listen to and value others' input?

Sometimes our best help is simple, unspoken support. But what if we have a sound, provable bit of information we very much want to offer a struggling friend who seems deserving and could surely benefit from the counsel we could so easily give him? How can we offer this in a way that will be most acceptable and least offensive? Coleridge offers this poetic suggestion we could all benefit from considering:

Advice is like snow; the softer it falls and the longer it dwells, the deeper it sinks into the mind.

HOW THE MASTERS HELP US – LITTLE MIRACLES

*We know that all things work together for good to them
that love God and are the called according to his purpose.*

Romans 8:28

Knowing how the Masters help us strengthens our faith. Lemurians often sense this help in ways that seem perfectly natural, often subtle, but sometimes very dramatic.

How the Masters Help the Fellowship

When we put up our first Fellowship buildings during World War II, you couldn't buy cement without a government priority. But an unexplained shipment to the local hardware store enabled us to build, years before this material was generally available.

In the 1967 Ramona wildfire, much of our property burned except for the homes and office. Looking over the smoking ruins, a staff member saw flame burst from the ground at a gasoline pump, and steeled himself for the expected explosion. Instead, he said, the flame was snuffed out, as though someone had blown out a birthday candle.

Forty years later, in 2007, the Witch Creek Fire swept through the Lemurian Fellowship's Gateway property, scorching the brush-covered hills and meadows all around us. At its height, the firestorm roared toward apartments the staff had just left to shelter in a more protected building. Fifteen-foot sheets of flame consumed the bank in front of the apartments as we watched with helpless dread.

We were sure our apartments were a total loss, but amazingly, they were untouched. Of fourteen buildings on Gateway, only one small shed burned and another was damaged. Hundreds of acres of sage and scrub looked like a moonscape, but our chapel, homes, shops, and community building survived.

How the Masters help Lemurian students

For a personal story from the 2007 fire, read our article, "Spiritual Help in a Firestorm."

A Lemurian student was working to improve people's lives on a small Pacific island. On the day a ship arrived to carry him to the main island of his district, he felt extremely tired. Noticing tiny red spots on his legs and arms, he was shocked to recognize scurvy. Vitamin C was vital to avoid a fatal hemorrhage, but none was available there. On the voyage to the big island he slept on deck, and woke next morning with a large bruise on the hip he had slept on. And a blood clot in his mouth! His blood vessels were beginning to leak and he was in mortal danger.

Reaching the main island, he stopped at the Post Office for mail. There was a package from home with a bottle of vitamin C he had asked his dad for months earlier, and forgotten about. It probably saved his life. But if the ship had not come on the precise day he realized he had scurvy, he might never have reached the post office.

The other day our treasurer went to the bank. Stopping first at another store, she was chagrined when the cashier there kept her talking for several minutes. When she finally reached the bank, she found it had been robbed a few minutes earlier.

These few examples show how the Masters help us just when we most need it, the timing of these "rescues" too perfect to be coincidence. Our lives have a purpose, and when we are sincerely trying to fulfill that purpose and help others in keeping with universal principles, we are helped. We are humbly grateful for this aid from these Great Ones and try to live in ways that will continue to earn their matchless guidance and support.

LEMURIAN HEALTH LESSON

*A man should never be ashamed to own he has been wrong . . .
in other words, he is wiser today than he was yesterday.*

– Alexander Pope

A crucial health lesson for us began with soreness in his foot that made it hard for my husband to wear shoes, or walk. Gradually this progressed to swelling, inflammation, and pain. My husband and I come from quite different family backgrounds where health is concerned. He is geared toward alternative treatments; I look more to traditional medicine. As his foot grew worse, seemingly by the hour, he went back over every health lesson he'd learned in his life and did all he could think of to deal with what seemed to be a simple infection. Every hour for two days and nights, he took a quantity of supplements and concoctions he expected would help. But the condition worsened.

One of the most important helps the Philosophy has been to me has to do with finding the balance between helping another, yet not interfering in his right to choose what he feels to be best for himself. I wanted to insist he get medical help but I knew what he did with his health had to be his decision. I felt I had to trust he'd make the right choice for him, and tried to have faith that it would work out. But I was so worried about it I went outside to a peaceful spot to pray. After praying I felt a quiet sense of calm. I went in the house and told him as simply as I could that he'd tried his best but I thought he should seek medical help.

At that point he agreed to go to the emergency room as his foot had turned a deep purple. The swelling and color were enough to surprise even the emergency room doctor, and it had become quite painful. We learned the infection was cystitis or erysipelas, from which people used to die before antibiotics, and after a strenuous course of these, the foot gradually returned to normal.

Recovery took a lot of time off his feet, though, and during this period of convalescence the two of us realized an opportunity to talk over many things we'd seemed not to have time for until then. It was a turning point in our marriage. My faith in the Lemurian Philosophy helped me step back and not try to force an outcome just because I felt it was right. And he says that because I didn't push too hard, not only was he able to accept my help more easily, but learn a lesson about the limits of his own knowledge, too.

We know much of the effectiveness of a treatment depends on how a patient feels about it, so it was important to believe in my husband's choice to do what he trusted and felt was right for him. We both gained a deeper appreciation of the value of the other's ideas, as well as the limits of them. And our marriage has been stronger for working through this experience.

Light in My Darkest Hour

My darkest hour began with the staccato tapping of a police officer's flashlight on my bedroom window at 4:00 a.m., triggering a growing dread as I hurried through the dark house to the door. Why weren't the dogs barking at the doorbell? The three of them were always there unless my husband had taken them for a drive. And where was my husband? Was he okay?

That was the question I asked the two officers at my door. Then a chaplain appeared behind them, holding a Bible. I knew the worst thing I could imagine had happened.

There had been an accident, the first officer said, and my husband had died at the scene. His and another car hit head on. They had to use the "jaws of life" to reach my husband, so the dogs were imprisoned in the car for some time after the accident. My Labrador had been badly injured and was at the animal shelter, but the other two dogs were so badly frightened that as soon as the door was open, they took off running.

I was stunned – in shock – yet strangely calm. I knew in that instant that my life had just changed completely. All my family lived 1,700 miles away, and without my husband and dogs, I had never felt so totally alone as I did at that moment.

The one thing I did have was the Lemurian Philosophy. I had studied the Philosophy for several years, so intellectually I knew I would have help getting through this devastating time. But I had no idea how deep my faith had grown, how comforting it was to be in touch with the Lemurian Fellowship and have their guidance and the benefit of all I'd learned that would be with me through this time. I turned to God and my Lemurian lessons and began to put one foot in front of the other and move forward. In my heart I knew I would ultimately be okay.

I needed courage to face life without my husband, whose love and support had sustained me through our 26 years together. I'd always been independent and taken care of most of the household duties, but now I wasn't sure I could live on my own – or if I'd have to move back to live with my family. I wasn't sure where to start with funeral arrangements, and so many other decisions I had to make filled my mind. It was overwhelming. So I took time to read the Philosophy, started a list and began to check off each task as I completed it.

The Philosophy taught me that everything happens for a reason we often can't fully understand at the time of crisis, but that I am *never* alone even in my darkest hour. The help of God and my Fellowship teachers sustained me through the months ahead as I faced the many ups and downs. Life brings some hard things, but having a deep feeling that all was well sustained me with a strength that to this day is hard even to put into words. I am so grateful to be a Lemurian.

(Note: This story is an example of the kind of faith and willingness to use the Lemurian Philosophy in our lives that is a requirement for earning a place in the Lemurian Order. The author is now a staff member at Gateway.)

We must let go of the life we have planned, so as to have the life that is waiting for us. – E. M. Forster

GREAT ONES' HELP IN TRAGEDY

*The best portion of a good man's life: his little,
nameless, unremembered acts of kindness and of love*

– Wordsworth

One of the immeasurable blessings of being a Lemurian comes in learning about the Elder Brothers, Adepts, and Initiates who help and comfort us from the invisible planes. Because we rarely know who may have been responsible for special help we have received in times of need, we often refer to the Great Ones as our benefactors.

Every sincere Lemurian knows of times when these more advanced human friends have assisted or protected us. Here is one student's especially poignant story, expressing her faith and deep appreciation for the help any of us can earn through our own efforts to follow universal laws and help our fellow humans. She writes:

I most definitely recognize the help being extended by the Great Ones. There are no coincidences. Very recently my stepson was killed by a motorist while riding his bicycle on a dark main road. My son died instantly. The motorist used his pickup truck to block anyone else from hitting my son's body and immediately called for help. I know he felt terrible and can't imagine living with something like that. There is a possibility the motorist might have been at fault but that is something we do not know and it doesn't matter to us at this point. My husband and I hold no ill feeling toward this man and did not pursue any litigation.

Soon after this, while we were driving down a dark street near our house, a bicyclist crossed our path; we could hardly see him with his dark clothing and the lack of reflectors on his bike. Immediately my husband thought of our son and how his accident happened. We pulled over and motioned the cyclist toward our car and he came over. My husband cautioned him to wear reflective gear and shared with him how our son had just been killed riding on a dark street a month earlier.

The cyclist, about our son's age, introduced himself and gently gave us his condolences, and then revealed that not only had he heard about our son's accident, but it was his best friend who had been driving the pickup truck. He told us his friend was very remorseful and in his own world of grief and guilt. My husband and I looked at each other and knew this was no coincidence; it was meant for us to send our prayers to him. We told the bicyclist to tell his friend that we didn't blame him and were very appreciative of his staying with our son in the aftermath of the accident. It was meant for us to alleviate his pain too and I'm sure the Great Ones made this possible. I feel very emotional just thinking about this.

OVERCOMING FEAR

Fear Attracts Its Object

If you are afraid of something, you give it power over you.

Moroccan Saying

One intriguing fact of life is how we can envelop ourselves in failure by trying to avoid it. We've heard that fear is right up there with love in its intensity and all-consuming effects. And the Lemurian Philosophy goes so far as to state that fear is our most powerful emotion, and that fear attracts its object. But such fear has to be experienced before we can fully understand its power and avoid drawing such negativity into our lives.

I discovered this one day when I was working alone in our crafts shop, finishing a wooden pedestal for a music stand. We had been advised that a reporter from our local paper was visiting Gateway to gather information for an article she was writing about the Lemurian Fellowship. I wanted to be working on this pedestal so, if she asked, I could tell her what I was doing and answer any questions she might have. But anxiety was building as I concentrated on my work more than usual, hoping not to make a mistake. But evidently, the hope that I wouldn't wasn't as strong as the fear that I would!

Very slowly, I routed out three equal-length grooves in the bottom of the pedestal where the legs would be attached. As I heard voices announcing that the visitor and members of the staff were approaching, I glanced down at one of the cut grooves, only to notice it was a half-inch longer than required! Anxiety was replaced by panic! How could I have made this simple, stupid mistake when I focused such time and attention on getting it done right? But there was no time to address this question as I tried to recover my composure and attend to our visitor as the group arrived. Somehow, I did, answering the few questions she asked.

Only in reliving this experience later did I realize that my intense concern about making a mistake actually created that very mistake. And as if this discovery was not devastating enough, I made another equally as important ….my concern was focused not only on avoiding a mistake, but also on how any mistake would reflect on me. So instead of providing an interesting and informative experience for our visitor to enhance what she might write about the Lemurian Crafts, I was worried mostly about myself.

I relive these lessons many times, hoping their message is slowly being absorbed. I try to envision what I want in my crafts work and my life and think less and less about what I don't want. I know that fear attracts its object, but so do confidence, hope, and love!

Power of Thoughts

After years of tranquility in my apartment, I thought I knew something about the power of thoughts to create the environment we want. But just then, I began to experience the insidious intrusion of fear and insecurity. Someone seemed intent on making trouble for me and the accusations were making my life miserable.

The trouble started with a call from the apartment manager complaining of noises from my apartment, day and night. He said it seemed to come from my high heels on my tile floor. Since I have neither high heels nor a tile floor, I thought this must be about a different apartment and would soon be resolved. But it wasn't. The complaints continued and gradually, I began to feel, somehow, "If I'm accused, I must be guilty!"

I found myself analyzing my every sound and movement. I even asked my visitors not to talk too loudly. At one point, I thought I had found the culprit: my typewriter! Its sound might be mistaken for high heels on the floor. But since I need to use my typewriter, I started looking for ways to muffle its sound. All this increased my stress.

It would have helped to know where the complaints were coming from, but the manager refused to identify the source. Soon enough, I came face to face with my accuser as I left the apartment to get my mail. She yelled insults at me while spewing out the same complaints the manager had related. From then on, she seemed to appear wherever I went. One night, awakened by loud noises, I opened my door to see what was going on, and there she stood, yelling at me again! I was alarmed enough to call security.

The manager tried to reassure me that the woman wasn't dangerous. She had dementia and wandered into the corridors sometimes and they were watching her. I wasn't reassured. The power of thoughts had me in its grip and I had become too afraid of what she might do next. It was almost unbearable to realize I had lost the wonderful feelings of security and well-being I had known for so long! How could this happen? Why did it? And what could I do about it?

Asking myself these questions reminded me of the power of thoughts for good or bad and my responsibility to control my thinking. And as I did, I began to see that my neighbor wasn't really the problem. I had yielded to fear. I knew then that if I didn't get a handle on my thinking, I would remain a prisoner of my own fears and imaginings.

So I concentrated on getting my fears in perspective while focusing on all the good in my life. As I began to think more constructively, my faith and confidence came back. I could even think more compassionately about this poor creature with her obsessive paranoia – her cross to bear – and how very much more fortunate I am. And soon after I began to regain control of my own mind, for whatever reason, the new neighbor moved away, and the tranquility I so treasured, returned.

What a testament to the power of thoughts!

How Illness Helped Me

Just when everything finally seemed to be in place in my life – a wonderful wife and family, my medical career where I wanted it to be, the good health to enjoy it all – I got a headache over my left eye. I'd never had headaches. An eye exam was normal, yet I had to rule out a brain tumor.

Fear gripped me when tests showed a sizeable mass. Surgery right away would be best, but I found excuses for putting it off.

As I gradually accepted this tumor as a real intruder in my life that couldn't be ignored, I came face to face with my real reason for postponing surgery – something might go wrong and I could become an invalid. Once I faced that, I could begin to cope. I talked over probabilities with my wife and surgeon, and with their reassurance, I was ready, but I never expected to look back later to see how illness helped me.

I knew spiritual preparation affects physical outcomes. Gratefully, I had Lemurian principles to help me prepare. I knew it was important to see myself whole and to pray for the outcome to be for my best good. Part of my preparation included staying positive and accepting that I am worthy of love and the help I was asking from God. What could I change about myself that would change my health for the better?

All through school, I'd worked hard to make the best grades. My self-worth was always tied to work, grades, and achievement. I've always worked 70-80 hours a week. How would I have personal value if the surgery uncovered something serious and I couldn't work?

Then I pulled myself back. I knew through my Lemurian training and experience that a balanced life is most valued – balance between family and work; between material needs and spiritual strength. Most of all, I knew God's love wasn't based on how many hours I worked. Neither was my wife's or children's. Maybe the deeper purpose for this brain tumor was learning this lesson, and I began to sense how illness helped me.

I pondered these thoughts as I went into surgery. I visualized being able to care for my patients and work in my garden. The surgery went well, but recovery held several trials. I had a small stroke that cost me the use of my left leg . . . but only for two weeks. Just as that seemed behind me, the doctor had to operate for a blood clot that could have taken my life or left me an invalid.

I'm almost back to my old self – I hope the best of my old self. I relied on my faith in God and my Lemurian training to think only of a positive outcome during this entire experience. I had the care and love of nurses, physicians, and physical therapists. My surgeon was always there to fix my medical problems, and I had the steadfast help of my Lemurian teachers and friends.

Through this experience, I came to look at myself more realistically, to see I have value even when I don't work 70-80 hours every week, and to accept the love of my wife and our children. It was there all along; I just needed to let it in. Most of all, I came to accept God's love, and to know in my heart for the first time, I am of value to God.

Stuck and Frozen by Fear

When our running club scheduled a trail run, it sounded like fun. I suspected it would cover some rough ground, maybe even a stream or two, but this unsuspecting runner was totally unprepared for bogs or the possibility of being stuck and frozen by fear.

I was ready for a hard race, but when we came across the first bog, I felt unsure how deep it was and whether I might lose my footing. I decided the best way to get through was to stop thinking and just keep moving. I followed two other runners and as we navigated the muddy mess we noticed movement in the mud. A large black snake began to surface but then disappeared back down into the bog. My speed picked up dramatically and next thing I knew the bog was behind me. Although wet, cold and covered in mud, it felt good to be back on dry terrain.

As we approached the last leg of the course, I was really looking forward to reaching the finish line when – you guessed it – another bog! I started through it but this one was larger and much deeper. Panic rose in my throat and I can still hear the sucking sound as I lifted each foot – not knowing if my shoe was still on.

Mired in mud up my calves, I got so rattled I stopped. Big mistake! I lost my nerve, stuck and frozen by fear in that bog.

It wasn't the idea of snakes that got me but fear of falling in the oozing muck that clutched at my heart. I looked in vain for a way out while trying to block visions of TV cowboys meeting their demise in quicksand. Fellow runners tried to encourage me to stop worrying and just follow them. But I was stuck!

What finally helped me set my paralyzing fear aside and deal with the situation was remembering what the Lemurian Philosophy teaches about the power of positive thinking. To overcome my fear, I visualized crossing the finish line. This replaced worried thoughts about falling into the mud. I could stop thinking of myself and focus on the unselfish kindness of those runners who were also wet, cold and tired but cared enough to stop to help me.

With their support, I managed to get through that bog and finish the race. I surely was a muddy mess but I didn't fall in. And I still had my shoes! Looking back on this experience, I realize my unfounded fear was paralyzing. Yet I was able to get past it and learn something. Now when I find myself in a difficult situation and there seems no way out, I can think back to how I overcame that muddy bog. It helps me to know I can work through a challenge and come out okay at the other end.

Beating Accusations with Lemurian Faith

Seeing the principal at the door of my orchestra classroom surprised me. She doesn't usually make "house calls," so I knew something unusual was up. But what she said really disoriented me: One of my students accused me of hitting her!

My head whirled, everything moved into slow motion as these words sank in. I tried to think what could have brought this on. Then I remembered the day before, Alexis kept playing her violin after I signaled the orchestra to stop. More signals and words had no effect, so I walked over to her and lifted her bow arm off the violin. That was the only thing I could think of that might have triggered this.

When I told my husband that evening, at first he laughed out loud, waiting for the punch line. But the following days were no laughing matter as the principal interviewed other students and my teaching assistant about what had happened. Meanwhile, Alexis kept coming to class, greeting me with her big smile as though nothing had changed. It was a little surreal.

The day came for our meeting with Alexis' mother.

The principal asked how I could stay so calm with this tornado swirling around me. Didn't I know accusations like this, even if untrue, could ruin careers?

I told her my Lemurian Training helps me know how to handle any situation, and that brings a sense of security.

My faith keeps me strong because I know what happens is for the best. I can't change what another thinks or does, but I can control my reactions. This gives a degree of serenity and personal power over whatever happens around me.

We watched Alexis' mother approach the school. She caught us off guard with a friendly greeting. Instead of being upset, she talked about her recent divorce and the fun things she and Alexis were doing together. When there was finally an opening, the principal brought us back to the reason for our meeting, and what she had learned from her interviews. They indicated there had been some contact, but no hitting. Even so, I was asked to apologize, and I did. Then the whole thing melted away.

In a surprise ending, Alexis asked to be in my class the next semester. I wonder if the accusation and the attention it drew were excuses for bonding between this daughter and her mother, or maybe a reaction to the difficult emotions of the divorce. I may never know for sure. But what's important is what I learned and the added layer of strength it gave my Lemurian faith.

My Brush with Death

A brush with death seemed unthinkable as I started a store on a lovely Pacific island. But I had a lot to learn.

Ships visited Ruo island every three months to buy the islanders' copra and sell food and supplies. Between ships, the people had no way to make money or buy goods, so they were eager to form a co-op. As members joined, we designed a building. Labor was no problem since the men often built basic, concrete homes. But cement and roofing were expensive, not to mention goods to stock our store, leaving little to pay laborers. Still, several members volunteered to work for the minimal wages we could offer.

All went smoothly as the building took shape. Then the workers' leader, Asauo, said the men wanted more money, or they would slow the pace of their work. This was a poser. The fledgling co-op couldn't pay more, but without a building, we'd have no store.

I tried to explain that all the co-op members were counting on the workers to get this venture going. Actually, they were the first members to benefit, by earning wages. They had agreed to the stipulated wages, and to demand more now would be in "bad faith." I had no idea how to translate this term into their language, but Asauo nodded soberly, saying "luku ngau," meaning roughly "bad thought," and seeming to understand.

The problem apparently resolved, the men returned to work, but the sweat I wiped off my face was not just from the heat. That night, though, matters took a chilling turn.

Asauo got drunk and tore into the taro groves with a machete. You could hear him crashing through the brush, yelling incoherently, nearer, then farther. Under local custom, people were not held responsible for what they did while drunk, and tales of what some islanders had done to others while inebriated were hair-raising. And I'd already had one brush with death when a drunken islander charged into my house, enraged about something that was never explained. Fortunately, he was closely followed by the island policeman, who wrestled him out the door again.

But no policeman was near on this night. And all that stood between the bellowing Asauo and me was a flimsy screen door.

Never have I been more grateful for my Lemurian training than during that long and troubled night. It assures us that when we do our best and ask for help, things work out for our greatest good. I was trying to help people improve their lives and not taking advantage of the workers but compensating them as well as I could. I hoped I had done enough good up to that point to offset whatever ill might befall me because of a disgruntled worker. Since worrying was futile, I tried to visualize success for our store, and eventually fell asleep in the wee hours.

The young man must have dissipated his unhappiness in the taro groves, for soon the incident faded from memory. Our co-op building was completed faster than we hoped and provided goods and salaries for the islanders during the years I lived there. My understanding of people grew from that experience too, as I realized how tricky it can be to work with others when there are language and culture barriers. But the workers and I became friends. And my faith in Lemurian principles grew stronger.

Bucking Family Tradition Was Best

Nursing wasn't my first career choice but I decided to try it at a college where my grandmother went and my grandfather had taught. Since medicine is the family tradition, to say they were proud and excited is an understatement, and since they were important to me, this felt good. But medicine wasn't a burning desire, just a natural choice. And the next year, I found my true calling. By this time, I'd studied the Lemurian Philosophy longer than I'd been in nursing school and I wanted to devote my life to others through the Lemurian Program.

After months of agonizing, I wrote my grandparents that I would leave school. They were clearly disappointed. My grandmother called with questions from my grandfather. When I asked to speak to him, she said she would relay my answers. Several letters and calls from her brought more questions. It was strange and intimidating, but knowing they were having a hard time with my decision and were concerned about me, I answered as best I could.

My growing understanding of cosmic principles already enabled me to handle the situation with my grandparents in a kinder, less emotional way than I would have otherwise. While I was sorry to disappoint them, I knew the decision was right for me. My philosophy confirmed that we must each decide the right path for us in life, not follow a path just because of tradition or others' desires. And there was more to it:

When you follow a path truly right for you, make your own decision based on your best understanding, it can help loved ones.

When I first read this concept, I was intrigued but had no experience seeing how it worked. Soon, this crisis with my grandparents demonstrated its truth.

Just then my grandmother's appendix was removed so she couldn't care for the house, cook, or do laundry. She asked if I would come for two weeks to help. Wondering how this would work out with the strain in our relationship, I went.

During my stay, little was said about my career change until one morning my grandfather asked me out for the day. He wanted to show me the hospital where he consulted, and take me to lunch. During those precious hours alone with this man who had always inspired admiration and a little intimidation, he explained how proud he had been of my following the family tradition.

After I explained why I changed course, he said he was very proud of my strength and maturity in not giving in to a couple of older, more traditional people who were thinking more of themselves than me. I didn't completely agree, knowing they were concerned with what was best for me, but I appreciated his saying this. It was a great day, and I had a similar talk with my grandmother, coming away feeling much closer to both of them. I am so grateful for the guidance of the Lemurian Philosophy that helped me work things out with my grandparents in a way truly best for all of us.

Surviving My Worst Embarrassment

I was horrified! Two dozen people watched as I was publicly ridiculed for an awful mistake in the middle of a courtroom trial. It was my worst embarrassment.

As a young, recently hired lawyer in a high-powered law firm, I had been tapped by my boss to be his "second" in this complicated case, a wonderful chance to prove myself to this respected attorney.

All went well until suddenly, it came to light that I had overlooked what was needed to admit a key document into evidence. My boss's arguments nearly won over the court, but the opposing party's objection prevailed. I paled, knowing the case might be lost. Our client would be rightfully angry. Months of preparation and thousands of dollars would spiral down the drain. My boss turned to me, loudly demanding, "How could you have done that?" and worse.

My promising career at this new firm seemed over with the likelihood I would be fired. The judge glared at me. I could feel the pitying eyes of attorneys and spectators boring into my back. If only the floor would open up and swallow me, I could escape this horrible failure! But there seemed no way of surviving my worst embarrassment.

When the court day ended, my boss could barely bring himself to speak to me. The other attorneys who had watched this drama unfold offered words of sympathy but these meant little. I was completely wrapped up in my worst embarrassment and the fear of what lay ahead.

What sustains us at such low points in our lives? What keeps us from putting our tail between our legs and slinking away or drowning our misery in alcohol or drugs? We reach deep into ourselves for every strong character trait we have to survive, but times like these call for more than we have and are today. They're growing times. I needed help and I turned to my spiritual moorings.

The Lemurian Philosophy helps us find good even in failure.

With positive affirmations, I tried mightily to overcome my fear and change my negative thinking. As bleak as things looked, I knew that controlling my feelings would be a step toward changing my environment for the better, hollow as this seemed then.

I faced the next morning with dread, but determination. The trial had to go on. My boss's anger had softened, and he encouraged me to find a solution to the problem. Still a prey to self-pity, I could barely appreciate his effort, but with his continuing encouragement, we worked together to overcome my mistake and discovered another way to introduce the key evidence. The tide of the case slowly turned in our favor. In the end, the other side settled rather than risk a negative jury verdict.

After the case ended, we talked over what happened and how the mistake came about. To my joyous surprise, my boss asked me to assist him on other trials. From that point forward, I emphasized the Lemurian virtue precision, making sure to dot every "i" and cross every "t." I knew there would be other mistakes, but that I could learn a lot from them. And this was the start of a long and successful career at this firm.

STANDING UP TO MY FATHER

One of the hardest things I ever did was standing up to my father and telling him he could not stay in my home.

I'd thought of courage as brave acts. But I came to see it as overcoming the fear of looking bad in others' eyes.

After I married, Dad asked if he could stay with my husband and me while he was in our area. It seemed only sensible, but I had mixed feelings. He was an alcoholic, and the effects of this were fresh in mind. I knew the worry and fear when a parent can't control himself, and his alternating self-pity and anger.

I decided he couldn't bring this problem into my home. I had to lay down one rule, hard as it was: he couldn't drink in my home or come home drunk. I rehearsed, gathered my courage, standing up to my father and explained this to him. To my surprise he agreed and I sighed in relief, naively believing that would be the end of it.

When my father came in later, the slurred speech and familiar odor told me he'd gone back on his promise. I was surprised, then angry. This parent had expected me to follow basic rules of consideration he and my mom taught us, and he was ignoring the rules. How could I possibly handle this? My hands trembled and I shook with fear. My dad had been very strict with us and until this moment, I always tried to go along with him to avoid his anger or judgment.

Now, struggling to stand straight as he sensed my displeasure, he was ready to fight. It was the moment I had dreaded since I let him stay. I knew what I'd asked of him was right, and now had to stand by this decision or things would get worse. So I spoke a quiet prayer, blurted that he was drunk and he'd have to go to a motel.

He was more than upset. He used every argument in his lawyer's arsenal, saying I was not upholding my Christian beliefs, he was alone and how could I turn him out? When he spoke of my beliefs, I felt an inner strength and knew in my heart I was doing the right thing. The Lemurian Philosophy had helped me deal with his alcoholism, not run from it, and now there was only one way to handle this very difficult situation, by standing up to my father. After a very tense moment, he left.

Later, Dad called to say he was proud of what I'd done. It would have been music to my ears if he'd been sober. But like so many times in my growing up years, he hadn't changed. Yet my life changed forever. I would never accept my father's drinking again. Until now, when I was afraid of what someone would think or say, or how they'd react, I'd bend the rules to avoid the upheaval I feared. But this experience helped me know I must do what's right, even if it brings the reaction I fear most.

My relationship with my father changed. Though we never talked about that incident, he has treated me as an adult ever since, and never again has he expected me to accommodate his drinking. Having the confidence I needed for standing up to my father opened a bigger door, too. Today, when I feel something is truly wrong, I am not afraid to stand up and say no, no matter who appears to be in charge.

VIRTUE

OUR FIRST LEMURIAN EXAMPLE – ROBERT D. STELLE

*It is not alone for us, but for humanity
as a whole that we are working.*

– Robert D. Stelle

Have you ever known a truly advanced human being? Seldom do we have this opportunity, since it's rare to encounter men and women of superlative ability and character, usually born with a special mission, often at critical times to lead us through desperate and dangerous conditions. George Washington, Abraham Lincoln, Gandhi, Nelson Mandela, Mother Teresa stand out, almost larger than life, driven by an urge to tackle some critical need, setting themselves and their lives aside for the good of others. Their intense dedication to a greater cause lifts them out of the mundane, into greatness.

Others are shining examples of human possibilities not even imagined possible before them. Helen Keller, who lived blind and deaf most of her life, led the way for many who are overcoming physical handicaps to accomplish amazing things today.

Anyone who aspires to greatness finds it intensely inspiring to be around such people, and it can be life-expanding. Think of those fishermen of Galilee who answered Christ's call to follow Him, and how dramatically their lives changed. Few are ready for the kind of sacrifices the Apostles made, but many are looking for something beyond the ordinary in life, ready to respond to the inspiration of exceptional people.

Lemurian students are privileged to know one of these unusual people – Robert D. Stelle, who founded our Fellowship. Though he passed on many years ago, we know him about as well as you can know anyone you haven't met personally. He is our first Lemurian example who lived the Lemurian Philosophy he taught.

You may wonder how we can know a man we haven't met. We study the Philosophy he wrote and use its principles every day. We never tire of reading about his adventures. And he himself wrote about a very early incarnation when he helped begin the world's first civilization in Lemuria, also known as the Continent of Mu. Through his descriptions and lively drawings, we visualize scenes he took clairvoyantly from the Akashic Record.

We talked with and learned from those who lived and worked with Dr. Stelle during his lifetime. They tell us that under the most trying conditions, he never lost his sense of humor. He was impartial and just with everyone. He made all his friends feel there was something admirable in them. No matter what may have been in his heart, he was always cheerful – a familiar twinkle of fun and good humor in his eyes. He was more enthusiastic about others' success than his own. He was too experienced with life to worry, too noble for anger, too strong for fear, too happy to allow the presence of trouble.

And today, the intense practicality, sincere desire to help, irrepressible sense of humor, hard-working, self-sacrificing, kind, dependable, deeply thoughtful traits we see in our friends are his qualities that make our life and work such a joyful experience.

By the way, Dr. Stelle would not be comfortable with so much being said about him. For all his unusual abilities and deep understanding of truth, he was a very humble man who did not expect to be remembered for his part in bringing Lemurian history and wisdom to us from the forgotten past. But because he did, we have its guidance and help to make ourselves and our civilization into something we can be proud of.

Love, he told us, is one of the most potent of all forces. Without it, nothing is very worthwhile. With it, almost everything is. None of us are the type who can be driven, otherwise we would be of little use in our work. We all will cheerfully do far more for love than would be possible for any other reason. With it, we vibrate in perfect harmony, automatically converting the electrons into power for the purpose behind what we are striving to do — and will do, providing we always keep our ultimate objective before us.

NOT-SO-RANDOM ACTS OF KINDNESS

Kind words are short and easy to speak,
but their echoes are truly endless.

– Mother Teresa

Many people talk about random acts of kindness, and their stories are inspiring. To quietly serve another person seems to amplify the good many times over, especially when it's widely shared on the Internet. I got to thinking about not-so-random acts of kindness that may be less often expressed but just as valuable despite their rarity.

My first inkling of this came in a store one day. I asked the clerk for an item I needed and he turned to get it for me. A man and his little girl stood next to me and as I glanced over I saw his face was beet red. Momentarily puzzled, I suddenly came to and exclaimed, "Oh my gosh. I am so sorry! You were here first and I didn't even see you!" He visibly relaxed. His face returned to a normal shade as he smiled and kindly said, "It's okay, no harm done." Who performed the act of kindness here? I'd say that patient guy led the way.

Another time, I pulled into a Post Office parking lot to drop letters in the mailbox near a woman in an SUV, and saw her cursing loudly and literally bouncing off the walls of her car in fury. I pointed to the mailbox and mouthed, "It's okay, I'm going over there, not parking." The seemingly wild beast of a moment before immediately relaxed. A not-so-random act of kindness but a focused one, easing someone's obvious pain.

Another instance caught me off guard. Actually I was shocked. Grocery shopping, I was near the end of the meat case checking prices when an exasperated voice said, "For God's sake, every time you move I've moved out of your way. But I'm not going to move again!" Wow! How did I completely miss this person and his courteous attempts to give me access to the meat counter, or his rising ire? I said, "Oh, wow, I am so sorry." He laughed then and said, "It's okay, I'm just having a bad day."

Being aware of the people around us seems so basic and ingrained in us that it's a shock to discover we've missed something so important to another person. But when we make a sincere connection with that person, it so often clears the air.

It reminds me of a time I was driving and some teenaged boys pulled right up behind me obviously wanting to pass. I couldn't do anything about it then, but as soon as I could, I pulled over. I thought they'd probably yell at me as they went by, but they didn't. They honked and waved, and as their car pulled next to mine in passing I saw them smiling and saying, "Thanks!" Wow! I know that according to universal law, what I give out will come back, but it can still surprise me when it happens.

These are some of the seemingly ordinary, everyday moments that are without price, when we can express a kind of connection that shows someone we value them, we're all in this life together. When we make this small effort that costs us nothing, they feel happier, relieved, less stressed, and whatever the problem was evaporates in the genuine caring of a thoughtful human exchange.

How to Build Integrity

When I became a Lemurian student, I was a successful lawyer in a fast-paced, high-energy, good-paying position. But the only thing that seemed to matter to my firm was the results I produced, and I had strayed from my moral bearings, not to mention Christ's Teachings and natural law. To address this predicament would take courage, a virtue I felt I lacked. How to build integrity became my focus.

I feared the changes I wanted to make in myself could jeopardize my job, but I knew pursuing higher values was essential to my personal growth.

So I looked for how to build integrity in my work while trying to meet the goals of my clients and firm, realizing I was not trying to change others, only myself. It was a lonely road at times, but grudgingly, my bosses accepted more of the new me. And holding to my values in even small ways brought a special feeling of accomplishment.

I made many mistakes. When I tried too hard, was too impulsive or "letter of the law," I found myself in hot water with my superiors. I got frustrated and angry about what I felt was expected of me. Sometimes my courage failed because I could easily imagine the worst possible outcome. When I stumbled, it was disappointing, but at least I was trying. I drew comfort and many practical techniques from my Philosophy, tried to remember that what really mattered was what I, not others, did, and didn't let myself feel overly discouraged.

Eventually I realized I was more successful with gradual and quiet efforts to change, not pushing. Instead of refusing to do something because it was wrong, it went more smoothly when I just said I was uncomfortable with the idea. Another helpful approach was to speak to my boss ahead of time about an upcoming problem and propose a mutually acceptable solution. But most often, my efforts were known only to me as I followed the thread of integrity through my workplace challenges.

Then came an offer to join another firm. I gratefully accepted, resolving to make truth one of the hallmarks of my new venture. As time passed, though, again I found myself wrestling with integrity. This concerned me because, as a Lemurian student, I had a growing understanding of what to expect from the impersonal operation of God's laws. When it was clear I could not resolve this conflict within the expectations of my job, it was time for some hard thinking.

I asked myself what I enjoy most about law. It's helping others. The people part is so much more satisfying than lawsuits over money. Knowing this, with my wife's support, I went into public interest law. My new job gives greater satisfaction and makes a difference in others' lives. And clients' heartfelt appreciation is a great bonus.

Now I know I can be a successful lawyer and stay true to moral values. I'm happier and work with a deeper purpose. And arriving home in a better mood is an unexpected benefit my wife really appreciates. It's not always easy to walk the narrower path in a world with the emphasis on material accomplishments, but now I know it can be done.

PATIENCE – THE POWER TO WAIT

But let patience have her perfect work,
that ye may be perfect and entire.

– James 1:4

An advanced truth student said the more he learned, the easier the basic facts seem and the simpler the virtues needed for advancement. He suggested *patience* be fully investigated — its far-reaching implications thoughtfully considered, and for everyone who truly aspires to advancement along the Path to try sincerely to cultivate it.

One of the greatest obstacles to success in any area is lack of patience. Americans are characteristically impatient. *"Right now"* seems our main desire, while quality, beauty, harmony and thoroughness come after speed. Look at the faces of those who pass you on any busy street, and you will see the indelible stamp of this false doctrine. Strained, unhappy, anxious, worried faces rush past in their mad dash from here to there. Why? What do we gain by it? No wonder some are so unhappy! And all because of a lack of patience, the greatest healer of all.

Too many people consider patience the same as passiveness, but they are very different. Patience is the power to wait calmly; passiveness is not acting, but being acted on. Think about these two definitions. Passiveness is truly negative — the "do nothing" approach which is the degeneration of patience.

Patience is an outgrowth of mind and soul. It is the power to wait calmly.

Endurance is patience plus physical and mental stamina.

Fortitude combines high courage with the habit and power of endurance.

Forbearance is refraining from an action that seems justified. It does not try to repay insult or injury, not from apathy, unawareness or passiveness, but by choice and the exercise of will. It is tolerance carried to the nth degree.

Patience and forbearance go hand in hand. They are the *sine qua non* of human understanding and kindliness.

When all else has failed, try patience. It will save you many heartaches. It will solve an unbelievable number of your hardest problems, and most of the time, is actually the shortest path to success. It will bring into your environment a peace that can be experienced in no other way.

The next time you have a tedious job, feel that some problem is beyond your comprehension, or somebody doesn't jump as fast as you think he should, try patience. The heat of the day will seem less unbearable, the trials and troubles that, like mosquitoes, seem to be driving you frantic, will disappear as when a cooling breeze springs up. Not only will patience restore God to His Heaven, but it will bring peace, contentment and happiness into your environment.

Who does not love the patient, kindly, tolerant person who is always forbearing, understanding and just? Who welcomes us with a heartwarming smile, and who patiently and with fortitude listens to our troubles while withholding any hint of his own?

– Robert D. Stelle

FIGHT OR FORGIVE?

Not long after moving to another area of the country together, my husband and I came to a parting of the ways and agreed to divorce. Like so many people in this situation, we had to decide whether to fight or forgive.

We had recently put a large down payment on a new living room set, and when we split our assets, I was given the furniture since it was too much for him to try to move any distance. We agreed verbally on dividing all we owned, without lawyers, as we had an amicable relationship in many ways.

As my now ex-husband moved back home to be close to his family again, there were many adjustments to make, including the fact that now, there was no one to share expenses with. So it was a shock a few weeks later to receive a notice from him that he wanted half the amount we had paid on the furniture returned to him, and felt I should pay him this amount.

When my ex-husband asked me to pay for half of the furniture we'd agreed I'd keep, negative, suspicious thoughts began to obscure the harmony we'd maintained.

This was dismaying from many angles, not the least of which was that I didn't have the money to pay him. I felt torn. Should I fight or forgive? While the down-payment money had come partly from an inheritance from his side of the family, on the other hand, in the years of our marriage I had worked full time so he could attend college and get his degree. I really didn't know what was fair or what to do.

I talked it over with my Lemurian Fellowship teacher, who helped me see that non-resistance was the best course. She explained that if I did pay him the money and it was rightly his, I wouldn't lose anything in God's eyes. And if I paid him an amount he was not truly owed, that too would balance out in the long run by the action of universal law. So I arranged to pay my ex-husband month by month, and he was agreeable.

I mailed the first check, and then a second one. But at that point, he called me and apologized for asking for the money. He felt it had been wrong to do so, and he sent my two payments back to me. We parted on good terms, each having thought about some of the good the other had contributed to our marriage.

I believe my faith in the Lemurian Philosophy allowed the time and space for both of us to thoughtfully decide what *we* really wanted, and not just react to the emotion of the time or pressure from well-meaning family. I gained a lot of respect for his integrity, and for the value of non-resistance.

Putting Lemurian Virtues To the Test

I manage properties for absentee owners in an upscale community. One client asked me to supervise a landscaping project and guesthouse remodel with a time goal. But he added, "As much as I like you, you don't have a mean bone in your body, and frankly I don't think you have what it takes to push these guys to make their deadlines."

"I'm a Lemurian," I said; "we're taught to lead by example. Who will do his best work, one who fears reprisal, or one who respects you?" "You have a point," he said, "but they may eat you alive!" I talked it over with my wife, knowing it would make many demands and I would need all the Lemurian virtues to pull it off. Then I accepted.

I hadn't worked in home construction recently, and codes had changed. So when the cement contractors arrived, I asked a lot of questions and expressed interest in their work. They spoke politely in English, but Spanish comments in the background were somewhat less polite. Having lived in Mexico, I understood but ignored these, bringing out a table for their plans, and as it got hotter, a shade umbrella. The background comments slowed, and when I began handing out Gatorade, they changed to good-natured ones like, "Where's the super? I'm thirsty!"

As new workers arrived, I told them, "We have a deadline no one thinks we can meet, so let's make it easy on each other. I'll do anything I can to make your job easier, so just work with me." They did. I provided work areas, power, water, garbage cans, shade, fans and drinks. I jockeyed vehicles around so they could load and unload tools and material, ran to get parts and materials, helped carry things, learned their names, asked about their methods and thanked them for their good work. Soon, if I got back late from an errand, I'd find the fences had been put up and locked, the road washed and the site cleaned. They would tell new people not to park on the north side of the street and did many other things to help me out.

When the owner came to check on us, he saw over 60 people setting tile, hanging doors, welding, landscaping, painting, plumbing. He agreed my method worked after all.

I asked if I could use his refrigerator to keep cold drinks for the workers. He thought it was a great idea and reimbursed me for the drinks. That bill was over $1000, but it was worth it. It was fascinating to see all those people from different trades stopping together to enjoy a cool drink; like sharing a meal, it creates a level of camaraderie that is sometimes rare on construction sites.

Trying to juggle my regular responsibilities with this new one seemed impossible at times, but except for a temporary rise in blood pressure, it was a great experience, stretching my capabilities. I tried to stay calm, cheerful, and approachable, and never yelled at anyone. The job was completed on time to everyone's satisfaction, a memorable demonstration of Lemurian principles in action.

Insightful Virtue Tolerance

There's so much good in the worst of us,
and so much bad in the best of us,
That it behooves the most of us to
get along with the rest of us.

– Anon

I'd been a Lemurian student for about a year when I began studying the Lemurian virtues. The insightful virtue Tolerance was one of them that I breezed through, pretty sure that was someone else's problem. Looking back now, I realize this opinion was a red flag indicating a need to look at things more carefully. But I was clueless then.

But I was learning a lot about myself and could recognize some areas I needed to work on and change. When I came to the part of the lesson that talks about the need to look back on our thoughts and actions to discover the learning they hold for us, I started thinking about a guy I used to work with. He was always joking around and making personal comments I felt were inappropriate. I considered him a loudmouth, a shallow person I didn't want to know. And that's how I treated him.

Eventually, our company assigned him to an overseas position and a little bit later, I went there on a business trip. He was the one assigned to sponsor me. "Oh Lord," I mourned, "What a trip this will be!"

Was I ever wrong! He couldn't have been more solicitous of my needs. He welcomed me into his home where I observed his heartwarming interactions with his wife and children. He was a gentle and loving man. My view of his public persona had led me to completely miss what a fine person he was.

I hadn't thought much about the fact that a lot of us act differently in public than we do at home. And it may have been that some other facet of his life had changed him; I don't really know. But if I'd used the insightful virtue, Tolerance, and observed this coworker more carefully, I might not have been so surprised at the apparent change.

Thinking back over this experience, I could see how snap judgments about people – based on my intolerance of ways different from my own – often caused me to miss out on good relationships. Too often, I exhaust myself stewing over some real or imagined wrong. Or worse, I might lose out on the best of all human experiences – gaining a friend.

Tolerance is a tough virtue to build into ourselves, especially when others might not seem to consider it worth a second thought. But for those of us who aspire to become finer, better, and nobler people, it's essential. What we learn by taking time to consider others' opinions can open up a whole new and better world for us. So how do we acquire it? One of the Fellowship teachers suggested an interesting way to start, saying,

Tolerance is pretending that opinions which disagree with yours are not nonsense.

THINGS OUR LIFE MISSES

I just got off the phone with the Dean of Instruction, and I was fuming.

The job I wanted – a job I had been doing unofficially for three years – had just been given to the other finalist.

The Dean said it had been a difficult decision as the two of us had very similar qualifications, but the other finalist had a little more experience with the software we would be using so they gave her the job.

I'd been working as a part-time instructor in a college lab, and since there was no full-time instructor, I had been running it myself. My supervisor often praised me for going above and beyond my normal duties, and everyone assumed I'd get this new position. But I didn't and I was bummed! All kinds of negative thoughts rampaged through my mind, keeping me upset and annoyed at this ingratitude after all I felt I had done for the college.

Next day I was still upset and didn't like this feeling. So I had a serious talk with myself. After 24 hours of feeling sorry for myself, the "pity party" needed to stop. I needed to get a grip. I had been studying the Lemurian Philosophy for years and knew it held the means for me to turn this around.

First, I believe all things happen for our greatest good. Hadn't I gone into each interview wanting to succeed, but also wanting whatever was for my greatest good? Second, while only time would allow me to understand why this position was not the best for me, now I needed to turn my thoughts away from myself and think about others. Doing this – being selfless instead of selfish – could help me overcome my negative emotions.

I thought about what a difficult phone call it must have been for the Dean to make. Yet, she was kind and thoughtful, thanking me for all I'd done for the college and hoping I would continue with my present teaching assignment. I knew such a call would have been very hard for me to make. So I decided to write her of my gratitude for her kindness. And doing this changed my negative feelings into positive ones and helped me feel better.

About two months later, a new opportunity came along and I realized not having a full-time job gave me time to work on things that were more important to me. And later, I had the chance to talk to the instructor who got the job, and as I listened to all the challenges she was running into, I could see clearly how all things did work out for my greatest good. That's when I thought of the lines from an old poem:

> *And sometimes the things our life misses*
> *Help more than that which it gets.*

> – *Nobility* by Alice Carey

Working for the Great Ones

A special tribute written by the Fellowship staff of the 1940s

Can you imagine the privilege of working for the Great Ones? We find a peace and tranquility in our work beyond our greatest hopes, beyond our ability to express. And we find in the others of our group the same hope that animates our own hearts.

Each of the Fellowship staff comes from a different background and environment, but all must live together in peace and harmony. This takes constant work on kindness, tolerance, sincerity and charity. The Golden Rule, moderation and balance are essential as each of us helps the others gain what's deficient in their makeup, just as they help us.

Much of our work is correspondence with our students, but there are also meal preparation, landscaping and care of the grounds, housework and maintenance. There are personal interviews and visitors who are extended every courtesy, the many details of bookkeeping, reports, writing lessons and articles, and much more. We must be versatile in our ideas, creative in our approaches, like clay in the hands of a sculptor, receptive to the molding of our lives as the pattern grows clear.

Some ask us about jobs like housekeeping, seeming to think this sort of service holds no opportunity for advancement. They don't realize we work at our self-selected tasks for the pleasure of serving, knowing we are working for the Great Ones to the best of our ability and gaining the spiritual advancement every Lemurian seeks. It doesn't matter *how* we serve. In the early years, the office staff contributed much of their precious time in canning fresh fruit and vegetables.

If you have a big family, you may know what it's like to have twelve or more for a meal. Our group comes from different parts of the country, with different eating habits and individual ideas. Yet, each fits into the group and becomes one great, loving family. To do this, we have to use all the virtues, or the harmonious, peaceful, and understanding consideration we enjoy would not be possible.

We have a most splendid example in our dear Dr. Stelle. We all turn to his ever natural and valuable counsel in our time of need. We have yet to find him too busy, impatient, or unwilling to help. He never seems to tire under his heavy burden, and we each try in our own way to repay him with the love and devotion he richly deserves. Maybe this will help you better understand the happiness and feeling of true brotherhood which makes our serving a source of endless joy, and helps our advancement along the Path.

Each day, as twilight beckons our family to the supper table, we find ourselves surrounded by smiling, happy faces, each a little more kindly than the day before, and each a little more appreciative of the others. I can think of no greater or more splendid wish for all who read this than that, someday, you too may find yourself in just such a haven of peace and loving understanding as our daily life here at the Fellowship.

We weave the thread of our desires into a pattern of beauty linking God, our brothers and sisters, and ourselves. This we gain from our work which feels like the velvety touch of Spring on the pure face of the apple blossom whose fragrance permeates the air so softly. And as evening shadows fall, a gentle breath of night air rustles through the trees and brings us closer to the time when all our dreams will become realities.

LEMURIAN LIFE

"What is a Lemurian?"

Eye hath not seen, nor ear heard,
neither have entered into the heart of man,
the things which God hath prepared for them that love him.

– I Corinthians 2:9

"What is a Lemurian?" We used to get this question a lot, but not as much now that more people are familiar with the term and have some definite ideas about it. Still, "Lemurian" means different things to different folks. We talk with people who have an innate feeling they once lived on the massive continent that long ago graced the area of the earth now taken up by the Pacific Ocean. Others express a mystical belief that somehow, they *are* Lemurian. And many of these people may be right.

To us, "Lemurian" refers to the inhabitants of Lemuria, or Mu, an ancient civilization of such antiquity that it's more a myth than a memory today. Its origin is thousands of years before commonly accepted history and predates even Plato's Atlantis. Its people are of great interest to us because they accomplished something no one else has come close to doing since — creating an organized and harmonious society that endured for 50,000 years. We learn of the beginnings of the Lemurian civilization and of the wise and highly advanced beings who guided it in Dr. Robert D. Stelle's book, *The Sun Rises,* revealed to him clairvoyantly from Nature's infallible Akashic Record.

Those of the Lemurian Fellowship, the Lemurian Order, and Fellowship students today are Lemurians because we study and try to live by the Lemurian Philosophy, the most ancient of all religious teachings.

We understand if you feel that a philosophy claiming to be based on such unconventional and seemingly mythical elements would be sketchy at best and delusional at worst. But you'd be mistaken.

Far from a figment of someone's imagination, fantasy, or science fiction, the Lemurian Philosophy is true, authentic, and thoroughly practical. Since the Masters of the *Lemurian Brotherhood* first began releasing these teachings to the public through the Lemurian Fellowship in 1936, thousands of students have studied and used its timeless principles to improve their lives, discover and fulfill their purpose in being on this earth, and make real progress in the pursuit of happiness, affirmed as a human right in the Declaration of Independence of the United States of America.

Dr. Stelle, Masters, and Lemurian Lives

Hawaiians of ancient times believed there was one great continent stretching from Hawaii as far as New Zealand.

– William Hyde Rice

Understanding the connections between Dr. Stelle, Masters, and Lemurian lives takes understanding reincarnation. Every time we come into a new life, memories of the past are veiled and we begin with what seems a clean slate. But we pick up our personal soul development where we left it, along with certain abilities, life lessons, and karma – good or bad. We meet those who can help us fulfill our purpose and those we need to work things out with. Observant, deeply thinking ones like Dr. Stelle soon begin to piece these clues together to understand who they truly are, and why they are here.

From early childhood, Dr. Stelle was able to see fascinating scenes from the Akashic Record, but didn't know how they fit together or what they meant. After being punished for telling what others thought were lies, he stopped talking about these visions, but kept thinking about them. At 12, he was contacted by a group of Masters who showed him many unusual things – again without fully understanding this was preparing him for a rare opportunity.

His early adventures, discoveries, and meeting with the Master in China (*Lemuria and Robert Stelle's Revelations*) only deepened his intense interest in Lemuria. He studied everything he could find about it. He began receiving new information from the Masters and came to understand he was being given a very important work to do. He was expected to transmit the legacy of this great civilization and train people how to use its forgotten wisdom for the good of mankind.

Dr. Stelle began to realize his visions were scenes and personal experiences from that long-ago time, and now he could see more. Along with his responsibilities as President, Counselor, and teacher of the Lemurian Fellowship, he began writing *The Sun Rises*, a history of how the world's first civilization was formed.

Since the Lemurian Fellowship began training students, many who were part of that ancient civilization have been attracted to the study. In this way, Dr. Stelle came to know the woman he had married in that long-ago life. They married in this incarnation too, and together carried forward the Fellowship's work. Other important characters from early Lemurian history reincarnated to help them.

Since that modest beginning in the 1930s, thousands of people have studied with the Lemurian Fellowship, improving their lives and those of others around them, beginning to approach their true potential as they take to heart and use Lemurian principles. But many thousands more are needed.

Today we hear from more and more who have a haunting feeling that they lived in Lemuria. Very likely they did, since that civilization lasted for 50,000 years. And most urgent for those who feel drawn to Lemuria now is to prepare ourselves to help counterbalance the wrong thinking and darkness overshadowing our world today. We have everything to learn from the wisdom of a culture that was able to sustain itself for so long! And as we do, we will be part of building a better world for humankind, fulfilling the Plan of the *Lemurian Brotherhood.*

How Lemurians View Reincarnation

*I look upon death to be as necessary to the constitution as sleep.
We shall rise refreshed in the morning.*

– Franklin

If I could only start life again . . . If you could, what would
you change? You'll have a chance to make those changes,
and any others you may want to try, because you *will* have
another lifetime. Actually, as Lemurians view
reincarnation, you've already had hundreds, if not
thousands of lifetimes on earth, and you'll have many more
before you fulfill your purpose here.

The first important truth Lemurian students learn is that
the purpose of human existence is to learn how to control
our lives and destinies. The first humans, ignorant and
innocent, could not possibly reach that goal in one short
lifetime, so God gave us as many incarnations as we need
to evolve mentally and spiritually as well as physically.

*Why is rebirth – reincarnation – an essential part of our
ongoing for so much of our time on earth?*

We genuinely want to learn how to help others in the
best ways, to be kinder and more patient under difficult
circumstances, and someday to become advanced to the
point where we can easily handle every situation without
anger, frustration, or hopelessness. Obviously, to learn all

the lessons human life can teach us will take many, many years. We don't yet have the understanding of health and the human body to prolong our lives much beyond a century, and few reach that age.

Also, many of us – though not all – gradually lose the phenomenal ability to learn and grow that we had as children. We seem to develop a tough, rigid shell as we age so that, like the cicada, we must eventually split that old casing and fly away in another form so our lives and learning can continue. Only by incarnating in a new body, with much of our past experience withheld from us, can we begin again to really learn and grow.

Yet we know this pattern of transition or rebirth is not the ultimate. As we learn more about life and how to live it properly, we are prolonging our lives and learning well into later years. A hundred years ago, life expectancy in the U.S. averaged 51 years. Today, it's 79, giving a newborn baby almost 30 extra years! And we're just getting started. As we uncover and accept the role our mind plays, and learn to use it for our greater benefit, each lifetime can be fuller and more successful in helping us learn the lessons important to us. Eventually, we will be able to extend our lives practically as long as we choose, making our progress much more rapid as the years out of incarnation – and in infancy and childhood – no longer interrupt our learning and accomplishment here.

The Lemurian Philosophy tells us of those who have already fulfilled their purpose here on earth, and learned everything human life is designed to teach us. They are known as Masters, or Elder Brothers, and they have gathered together into Brotherhoods so they can most effectively work together to help the rest of us reach our ultimate goal, too. (While not all are male Egos, those of this development chose the term Elder Brothers as a way to help us view them as friends who love us.)

Mastership is far in the future for most of us, but even now, we enjoy many advantages that people have made possible through their unusual personal growth and creativity. If we think of the prehistoric cave man who lived a short, brutish life struggling to survive, we can be very thankful for the many aspects of intelligence people have developed over countless centuries that bless us with the comforts and pleasures of our lives today.

Why is it taking us so long? God also established universal laws or rules to be followed to keep all things in balance. Those who follow these rules succeed in what they attempt, and move steadily toward their life's goals. But doing what's right doesn't seem appealing to all of us and we don't always want to follow these laws. Instead, we choose objectives that are not in harmony with life's purpose or the laws of the universe, and we fail to progress, or even lose advancement we had made.

Can I come back as a flower or a dog? A lighthearted idea, but that's not reincarnation, it's *transmigration,* the belief that we can be demoted to animal or plant form in our next life. We are human, and we will return as humans until we either reach life's goal, or fail to. The rewards of human advancement are great; the pain of avoiding life's purpose is agonizing. Which will you choose?

Transform Your Life (A Soldier's Story)

At nineteen, I left college to join the army. My knowledge of war ranked right up there with my knowledge of space flight, but no problem for a teenager. At first, the physical activity and camaraderie were a little like going out for football, while death seemed remote, unreal. But as basic training progressed I became uneasy.

Taught to kill an enemy, it seemed clear I was not so much a person as a set of skills with but one purpose. If I was going to take life, or lose mine, what was the purpose of life?

One day during training a thunderstorm came up. As I enjoyed the lightning, high winds and hail, the big military machine around me shuddered to a halt – helicopters grounded, trucks pulled off roads, men running for shelter, everything stopped – and I felt the first joy I'd known in months. Something was mightier than the military, and it started me thinking about God.

I read about philosophy and religion – interesting, but vague. I wanted a way to use the ideas presented. So I turned to the spiritual teaching of the Lemurian Philosophy my parents studied and I grew up with. Since the Lemurian Fellowship offered a money back guarantee, I enrolled. It made sense – practical instruction on spiritual principles that can transform your life. There were fascinating facts about ancient civilizations, universal laws,

God's Plan for humanity, and God's helpers – advanced beings we know as Angels and Masters. When I had trouble understanding or using a principle, I could write the Lemurian Fellowship.

These universal laws quickly began proving themselves. I could see their effects on people and relationships around me and I could make them work for me. It felt good. I started looking outward and life became interesting again. I fully intended to honor my commitment to the government, but I found that knowing how to live in accordance with God's laws is more important than what we do in life. Instead of pushing to be a warrior, I decided to make the best of whatever lay ahead, learn from it and try to get out alive.

With basic training over, we were off to the war zone. It was strange to board a passenger jet as though going on vacation, and twenty-one hours later see the plane's lights extinguished as the dark airfield came into view. From a midnight landing in the sand, we were rushed into armored vehicles for a wild ride to the base, which brought the first pangs of fear.

The next 18 months brought a new appreciation for the Lemurian Philosophy. Studying whenever I could built inner peace that allowed me to accept and even look forward to whatever came. Though my job working on tall radio towers put me in mortal danger, worries dissolved. I could empathize with the suffering of the people as well as fellow soldiers drowning their fear in alcohol and drugs.

I was sure my life wouldn't end there and another purpose awaited me, but I wasn't foolhardy about it. When others seemed almost paralyzed by fears, my own were fleeting. I was too busy trying to understand myself, improve my actions, looking toward a brighter tomorrow.

[Another brighter purpose did lie ahead. The author later became President of the Lemurian Fellowship.]

PEACE AT GATEWAY, LEMURIAN ORDER HOME

*What is happiness except the simple harmony
between a man and the life he leads?*

– Camus

The property selected by Dr. Stelle and approved by the Elder Brothers in Ramona's Valley of the Sun is off the beaten path, tucked back against rolling hills in a quiet rural setting. Since 1954, it has been the home of the Lemurian Order, known as Gateway.

For over sixty years, with the Lemurian Fellowship's patient guidance, the Lemurian Order has worked to create what Dr. Stelle termed "the ideal life," in which the well-being of others is as important as our own. Lemurian life is based on the laws and principles that made the Lemurian civilization an outstanding success, and stresses cooperation, consideration, and mutual respect. To the degree all involved adhere to these ideals, it infuses a growing feeling of security and purpose rarely found in the world today.

When anyone works hard to create harmony and peace, this effort can be felt in their environment. And when many people work together to realize these spiritual blessings over a period of years, their community gradually takes on the higher vibration we associate with true spiritual living.

Eventually, this becomes palpable enough that people begin to notice it.

Those of us who live at Gateway sometimes take its tranquility for granted, but seldom do we drive in the entry road that we don't feel the cares of the world begin to slip away as our eyes light on a spread of purple fillaree, or the chuckle of a meadowlark soothes our ear. For some of us, the sense of peace starts with the coruscating colors of the dawn sky or an especially clear rainbow. Or it may be the bass chorus of bullfrogs after a rain, or the warble of five or six coyotes vying to sound like a dozen.

For students and Order members who visit Gateway, the contrast to their normal lives is usually sharper. One recent visitor said, "I felt the need to put aside some of the more vexing problems and allow situations to be as they are without interference. It is nice to let go and relax when resting in a grove of trees with the wind blowing softly and the leaves rustling, each bird song adding beauty to this scene of tranquility and peace."

Another said, "When we walk the land on a quiet day, with the breeze nodding the flowers, and with sunlight and shadows playing on the grass, there is a continuity of peace each of us can carry away to our separate lives, that can bring us together in reflection and meditations, or in time of need."

And when strangers, unacquainted with Lemurian ideals and unaware of Gateway's purpose, comment about what they feel here, it's always gratifying, an indication that we are succeeding at what we're trying to accomplish. Often, a contractor will pause while installing a water heater or repairing a phone line to say, "You really have a peaceful place here." And not long ago, a delivery crew brought a new mattress that was scheduled to arrive in the afternoon. They didn't make it until after dark and they were all tired and in a hurry to be done by then. Yet, the one who carried the mattress in paused a moment to say, "It's really peaceful here."

It really is.

THE LONG GOODBYE

> *"The souls of the righteous are in the hand of God,*
> *there shall no torment touch them. In the sight of*
> *the unwise their departure is taken for misery and*
> *their going from us to be utter destruction,*
> *but they are at peace."*

– The Wisdom of Solomon

Why did I think, when my mother went on hospice, that it would be like the movies or TV? The fading loved one, pain-free as morphine gently drips from an IV, the family gathered around saying goodbye, it's okay to let go, we'll be all right. The last slow breaths and it is over. About as unrealistic as expecting a Facebook profile picture to resemble the real person. The long goodbye was only beginning for us.

As a Lemurian teacher, I work with students going through end-of-life experiences. Yet I didn't fully realize how long and complicated this process can be, even in its simplest moments. Death is as individual as the unique person going through it. And though Lemurians have a deep understanding of and respect for death, or *transition,* we still grieve the loss of someone we love, even if they have not yet departed.

Dementia is often called "the long goodbye" and it surely is. Ours began with Mom's moderate cognitive impairment and physical difficulties. When she suffered kidney failure, with the advice of the medical personnel, my sister and I found a way to gently speak with Mom about moving to a care facility and going on hospice. This face-to-face acknowledgement of impending death is a shock, yet Mom was okay with this and even grateful, and handled the move with grace.

As time marched on, unfortunately so did the dementia, weakness and mini-strokes, leaving her unable to convey her thoughts. She tried and we tried but, unable to make herself understood, this kind, friendly person gradually withdrew. In unexpected moments, in her anger, she didn't seem herself. But think of the deep frustration of being unable to make oneself understood!

Mom declined for years. We could no longer take her for a drive, she became bedbound and stopped eating. We prepared for the end and said our loving goodbyes. But after some days she began to eat again, even though unable to feed herself, needing bed baths and skin care. Sometimes she'd stare off into space. Other times she'd say her father (who passed in 1989) was there. At one point she seemed to go "out" for a bit and was sad to return to her confined existence. But more months went by and she just grew weaker day by day. She's been at the end of life for over six years. This brings mixed feelings that there is seemingly no end, yet grief that soon she will be gone.

Without our Lemurian Philosophy, this would be an almost intolerable situation. But we have practiced finding the good in every circumstance, even seemingly hopeless ones. It's always there somewhere! And we've used this time wisely. My mother has her affairs in order, and we have talked about transition, our love for one another.

Our understanding of reincarnation is a great comfort. We may feel so close to this person not only because she is our mother in this incarnation, but we may have lived other lives together too. And we know this life is not the end but only one chapter in a large book of our experiences on earth. In comparison to the lives we have already lived and the many ahead of us, this one is a passing moment and its difficult times will soon pass.

We also know we each have a purpose to fulfill that we decided upon before this lifetime and until that is completed, we are not ready to leave this life. Is that why Mom still holds on? Some karma from another lifetime she wants to work through now to free her for a more uplifting next lifetime? Isn't this her life alone -- between her and God? We may die with family all around us, but death is still a very personal moment. Yet as Lemurians we know that loved ones who passed before, and Egos of higher advancement, are there to take our outstretched hand as we let go of the earthly ties and return to a familiar astral home. We've all been through transition many times before. We can know our loved one is okay, at peace and in good hands.

It's difficult to live through the long goodbye. We probably won't know when the end is near. It has seemed near so many times and she bounces back. But we do know we've said all we wanted to be sure we'd said. We no longer say goodbye. We just visit, hold her hand, tell her news we think she'll understand, kiss her and trust she is well cared for and in God's hands.

As Lemurians we are keenly aware of not wanting to intrude into the choices and life of another person. So our prayers are for his or her greatest good, not for specific outcomes. But when we do pray in this way it is saying to God, "Thy will, not mine." When it comes from our heart it truly brings a measure of peace.

Seeing Death Differently

*Even in death there is much to make
one happy if he will but seek it.*

– The Secret of Happiness

Today we are almost bombarded by reports of death -- often unhappy, traumatic, even violent endings of lives that can be troubling to learn about and are so very far from the natural transition from one aspect of life to another that will be the experience of most of us. Here is another Lemurian's experience with and growing understanding of this change of life that almost all of us are destined to go through.

My uncle died suddenly when I was nine. At the funeral we sat listening to the minister as my cousins cried quietly around me. Though I barely knew my uncle, sadness pressed hard on my eyes and the back of my throat. No one talked to me about what had happened, what it meant, or how they felt. And I didn't ask. After the funeral, we went on with our lives as usual.

I was in college and a Lemurian student when my grandfather died, just as suddenly. I found my grandmother sitting in quiet shock and somehow smaller in her living room, relatives arranged supportively around her. Neighbors brought food. We ate together, visited the mortuary to view the body, and again there were waves of emotion but except for a minister's gentle words over the casket, no significant conversation. But by then I was seeing death differently.

My grandmother was not Lemurian, but because her son and his family were, the Lemurian Fellowship sent her a card of support. It was the one thing she seemed to respond to that day, wanting to know who sent it, saying how kind it was.

When my dad and I were alone that evening, he opened up in a way he rarely did, saying his father felt deeply about things, but seldom expressed his feelings. I knew my dad was talking about himself too. The powerful bonds of emotion and memory that connect us to a parent melted his own natural reticence. We had a free-flowing exchange about Dad's early life and our memories of grandfather. It was one of the best talks we ever had.

We remembered how capably he provided for his family, running a real estate agency in town while raising cattle, sheep, chickens and bees on the farm. His garden with seven-foot corn and luscious Concord grapes. How he lived twice as long as his father and brother, who both died at 40, yet how he worried about the heart attack that finally ended his life. How he always put up the bag swing and bought cases of soda when his grandkids came for the summer. We laughed at his famous absent-mindedness and the time he drove halfway to town before turning around to get his forgotten hat because otherwise, he said, "They'll think I'm a college boy!" Or the time he asked my mother if she wanted to go with him to town. She said yes, and he promptly drove away without her!

As Lemurians often do, we thought about what my grandfather may have wanted to accomplish during the life he had just concluded. We knew this was not the end, only one chapter in the great book of his adventures on this earth. He would be back someday to start a new life in a new body, and though we would miss him a lot and both thought we could have done more to tell him how much we loved him, there was no sense of loss or hopelessness.

Sometimes the full glory of a life is revealed only at death. The sadness of parting is natural, but very often we can see it as a celebration of a life well lived.

A life is fully known only to each of us and God, but from all we know about a loved friend, we can learn about life and ourselves.

ASTRAL PLANE, ASTRAL PILOT?

A merry heart doeth good like a medicine.

– Proverbs 17:22

Conversations About the Astral Plane

A good friend died suddenly while on vacation, which came as a shock. He was my first friend in my new profession, helping me immeasurably as I started my practice. So I kept busy trying to repay his kindness by helping his wife as much as I could.

After several days things settled down. At dinner one evening, I was suddenly struck with just how much I was going to miss Dan. We had talked often, gotten together for lunch every week and now, I realized, those times were gone. I started to cry.

My wife came around the table to give me a hug and some comfort. During all this, I was acutely aware that my four-year-old son, quietly eating and seeming to ignore us, was very much aware of what was going on. Knowing I needed to address the cause of my tears with him, I asked if he knew why I had been crying. He nodded. "Because Dr. Dan died."

"Right," I said. "But he didn't really die, did he?"

"No, he didn't."

"Where did Dr. Dan go?" I asked, welcoming this teaching opportunity with my son.

"To the Astral Plane," was his answer. (In the Lemurian Philosophy the Astral Plane corresponds to heaven/hell.)

"Right. Good job!" My heart swelled with pride and gratitude as a myriad of thoughts flashed through my mind. How wonderful it was to be teaching universal principles to him at such an early age. How the truth of reincarnation would simply be part of his consciousness; how he'd grow up with an understanding of truth from the beginning of his childhood. He was a new Lemurian in the making!

My reflections were suddenly interrupted as he brought me back to reality. I could almost see his little mind churning as he asked the question he must have wondered about ever since we began teaching him about death and reincarnation:

"Dad. Who's FLYING the Astral Plane?"

POWER OF OBSERVATION

I have yet to develop many aspects of true *observation* and I hope this mundane example will help explain what I mean. I've always loved working on cars, and learned enough to find a job in an auto shop. I think I'm reasonably observant in this area, but a mechanic friend, James, has developed *listening* into a fine art and a great example of the power of observation.

A customer brought in a car that he said was making a "screeching noise" from the front every once in a while, and left it for repair. James looked at it right away, figuring it might show the symptom more readily while it was warm. I started offering suggestions – a slipping belt, bad bearings, air conditioning clutch. As I talked he raised the hood and checked belt tightness, eliminating that. Then he started the engine and revved it up. I listened, but could tell nothing over the noise.

James got a stethoscope and listened at several points as he revved the engine. To my amazement, he turned off the engine and said it was a bad bearing in the air conditioning compressor. I asked him how he reached this conclusion so quickly and why he was so sure. He had me put my hands on the front fender where he had leaned over the engine and revved the motor again. After several tries I noticed a subtle vibration through the fender when the engine revs were falling, not rising. He gave me the stethoscope and had me listen again. I heard the air conditioner compressor make a different noise just as the vibration came on.

James had saved the customer the cost of a compressor and clutch, as only the front bearing needed to be replaced. I thought a lot about this demonstration of *the power of observation*.

James was always a step ahead of me at work. I put it down to his experience, but I was missing his power of observation!

I tend to use the shotgun approach to car repair, eliminating a range of problems one by one. This works, but takes lots more time. James was like a marksman with a laser-sighted rifle on the problem, his eyes, ears, and mind all engaged at once. Experience helped him, but he always quizzed his customers about their car problems thoroughly before he offered any solution, and sometimes not even then, while I jumped to conclusions that may or may not turn out to be related. It made me think about what more I might see if I listen.

[The Lemurian who wrote this story rightly attributes several important character traits to his mechanic friend. And he modestly downplays his own skills in comparison. We happen to know he is a very good mechanic in his own right, as well as a sought-after repairman, but the quality that really stands out in this story is his appreciation for another's power of observation and willingness to learn from it.]

RESOURCES

Brennan, Deborah Sullivan. "Mastodon bones place humans in America 130,000 years ago." *The San Diego Union-Tribune*. April 26, 2017. Retrieved December 13, 2019, from: https://www.sandiegouniontribune.com/news/environment/sd-me-mastodon-bones-20170425-story.html

Lemurian Fellowship, revision March 11, 2019, in *Wikipedia*. Retrieved December 13, 2019, from: https://en.wikipedia.org/w/index.php?title=Lemurian_Fellowship&oldid=887286878

Melton, J. Gordon. *Melton's Encyclopedia of American Religions* (Eighth ed.). 27500 Drake Rd., Farmington Hills, Michigan 48331: Gale, Cengage Learning. 2009, p. 708.

Rice, William Hyde. "The Menehune, A Legend of Kauai." *Hawaiian Legends*. Bernice P. Bishop Museum Bulletin 3, Honolulu, Hawaii. 1923, p. 33.

Wootson Jr., Cleve R. "Maya civilization was much vaster than known, thousands of newly discovered structures reveal." *The Washington Post*. February 3, 2018. Retrieved December 13, 2019, from:

https://www.washingtonpost.com/news/speaking-of-science/wp/2018/02/03/mayan-civilization-was-much-vaster-than-known-thousands-of-newly-discovered-structures-reveal/